OUR SOCIO-ECONOMIC ORDER

MUFTI MOHAMMAD TAQI USMANI

English Translation
by
SHAKIR RIZWANI

Prophetic Economics

Prophetic
Economics

Prophetic Economics Edition

Find our titles on your favourite online bookstore using the keyword 'Prophetic Economics'

Translation of the Qur'ān

It should be perfectly clear that the Qur'ān is only authentic in its original language, Arabic. Since perfect translation of the Qur'ān is impossible, we have used the translation of the meaning of the Qur'ān throughout the book, as the result is only a crude meaning of the Arabic text.

Qur'ānic verses appear in speech marks proceeded by a reference to the Surah and verse number. Sayings (Hadith) of Prophet Muhammad (saw) appear in inverted commas along with reference to the Hadith Book and its Reporter.

Contents

Foreword

For the past twenty-three years, I have been writing on the new problems that keep coming up in our present age and their solution. Most of these thoughts have been published in the monthly Al Balagh. Fifteen years back a collection of these articles running over 750 pages was published under the title, Asr e Hazir Mein Islam Kaise Nafiz Ho. (How May Islam Be Implemented in the Present Times).

Later, I had occasion to write on other aspects of the same topic and my friends, desired that these should also be included in the same book but as this would make it too cumbersome to benefit by, I decided to publish them in a separate volume. Besides, as the articles dealt with different subjects, such as politics, law, education, personal reconstruction, etc, a reader interested only in one of them would have to purchase the larger edition.

Accordingly, I have prepared separate volumes for different subjects. They are: -

- Implementation of Shariah and Connected Problems;
- Islam and Present Day Politics;
- Islam and Modernism;
- Our Educational System;
- The Individual's Reconstruction;
- A Life of the Holy Prophet ﷺ;
- Social Reconstruction;
- Our Socio-Economic Order;
- Muslims and Qadianiet.

Of these nine collections, the present one is Our Socio-Economic Order, I pray Allah that it may prove useful for Muslims everywhere, and for this humble servant a source of salvation in the Hereafter! Aamen!!

Muhammed Taqi Usmani,

3 Zil Haj 1410 AD.

Our Socio-Economic order

The socio-economic structure of a society may be described as satisfactory only when all the necessities of life, together with mental peace, are available to every individual. If the national produce is abundant, everyone shares the abundance, none should have any complaint about the unfairness of its distribution. But should the national income be concentrated in a few hands while the majority go hungry and poverty-stricken, pile upon pile added to the coffers of the rich, but the poor man's pocket drained out of the last of its pennies, then, even if the earth spit out gold and the machine produce industrial jewels, the nation cannot be described as progressive. This is the bankruptcy from which the nation can never emerge.

It must be the curse of our misdeeds that the economic feature of our society has become static: prima facie it would appear that in the twenty-six years after Pakistan was made, when we had nothing and had to begin with scratch, we developed our agriculture, industry and trade very considerably, and by Allah's Blessings, today we have everything. But the wealth has enriched only a few while the common man has not benefited in the least; to fill the starving body he has to labour more than ever before. Glitter of our wealth does not brighten his gloomy but, his days and nights pass in greater hardship and misery.

Why did this happen? The answer is quite clear. Since long there prevails in our society a semi-feudalism and a semi-capitalist system. Two-hundred years of foreign domination has so moulded our thoughts that instead of thinking out our problems independently, we have shut our eyes and continue to follow the road marked out by it. As in the other spheres of life, our economic structure too is built on the foundations which were raised by our feud-o-capitalist rulers for their own society. What could we, then, get, is evident, anxiety and failure that are inseparable from feud-o-capitalism.

After a bitter experience of many years, we are just beginning to realize that the road we have taken is that of ruin, not of progress. Most of us have been compelled to conclude that our economic dis-equilibrium is due to our capitalist structure cum feudalism. The pity, however, is that our minds are not yet so far liberated from the mental attitude moulded by the West as to carve out an alternative path, after having experimented with the crookedness of the foreign way of thinking. Instead, what we are doing is to turn to the West itself for solving the difficulties arising out of capitalism and refuse to accept any solution that does not come out of the West's thought-machine!

Today, some of us are turning to "socialism" and "communism", although both these thoughts are products of the same materialist civilization of the West, which gave birth to capitalism. The truth is that the solution for man's economic problems is neither with socialism nor capitalism. If the one is inflation, *afrat*, the other is deflation, *tafreet*. If labor and the peasantry were victimized under capitalism, they are nonetheless under communism.

The capitalist structure is based on the concept that the capitalist is the absolute owner of his capital and his ownership of the means of production is unrestricted. He can use them as he wishes, take as much profit as he likes, fix whatever price he deems proper, employ labour on whatever terms he is pleased with. In short, that he is at full liberty in respect of his trade and government must not interfere therein. But government does interfere and place certain restrictions on it. Nevertheless, the concept prevails that in spite of the restrictions, the capitalist "owns" the capital and creating capital out of his capital in any manner whatsoever is permissible. Accordingly, interest, (simple or compound), gambling, speculation, and hoarding are looked upon as the four pillars of the system, the evil consequences of which are before our eyes everywhere. Circulation of wealth has become increasingly uneven and unbalanced. By means of speculations, interest and hoarding, the capitalist accumulates wealth, and commands the market on the basis of this wealth. Prices are increased and reduced by artificial means; unnecessary, even detrimental consumer articles are brought in for trade and scarcity of the necessary commodities in manipulated. It has been seen that when the masses are in dire need of food, shiploads of wheat-grain and the like are sunk on the high seas, the storehouses are burnt down only so that the prices do not fall below the mark set by the capitalist. The food, then, does not reach those who are in need of it.

When such practices are rampant, the common man is unable to cope with them. His income remains limited while his expenses keep on the rise and his life becomes subservient to the countable few. The effect of the concentration of wealth is not confined to social economics but extends over social ethics and way of thinking, and national and international politics as well.

Socialism is at the opposite extreme. It pinpoints the defects of capitalism but provides no alternative solution. Capitalism believes that the individual is the owner of the means of production, while socialism says that he owns nothing; everything at his disposal should be taken away from the capitalist, and a committee selected from among or elected by the working classes should take over the management of all land and industry. This committee will apportion the work to the workers and decide what to grow or manufacture and distribute the income according to the ratio it decides upon.

This system is looked upon as providing a cure of all the ailments of capitalism, but the result has been that it has created new problems and the condition of the working classes has become worse, or continues, more or less, to be the same.

For the moment, we shall not consider the practical difficulties in the way of implementing such a socio-economic systems nor the fact that such a system cannot work except under a very severe dictatorship; or that labour and peasant are forced to work on things not suited to their liking or natural talents; nor that labour is forced and subjected to persecution; nor, yet, that religion and ethics are destroyed. We shall only consider how much of the national wealth reaches to the common man, peasant or labourer; in whose name this whole structure of socialism is built.

Those in authority comprise not even five per cent of the labouring classes, and they are not angels sent down from heaven. This group may be just as unfair to the workers' rights as the individual capitalist; if the individual capitalist can be tyrannical over his employees, so can this group which controls all the land, industry and wealth of the whole country.

No doubt under Socialism a number of individual capitalists are abolished but they are only replaced by one giant capitalist who does what he wills with this enormous capital. Therefore, a very small percentage of the national product is distributed among the workers and by far the greater part is left to be disposed of by the rulers. The outside world sees that the socialist countries are sending their satellites into space, but only a few people think of the price being paid by the workers for these adventures and how little they get of the wealth of their country. Just only a few prosper under capitalism, so as in socialism. Under both, the worker gets only what the few "masters" desire to give him. But under capitalism he can at least go on strike and protest in various ways; in socialism, he is not permitted to complain or voice his grievances in any way.

As opposed to both these systems, the Islamic principles of social justice trace a middle track between the two. Islam holds that it is not man but the Creator Who is the Absolute Owner of all the earth and the heavens and all the wealth therein, whether in the form of money or goods.

﴿لِّلَّهِ مَا فِي ٱلسَّمَٰوَٰتِ وَمَا فِي ٱلۡأَرۡضِۗ﴾ [البقرة: 284]

"Whatsoever is in the heavens, or the earth belongs to Allah". (Baqarah-284).

﴿ إِنَّ ٱلۡأَرۡضَ لِلَّهِ يُورِثُهَا مَن يَشَآءُ مِنۡ عِبَادِهِۦۖ﴾ [الأعراف: 128]

"Without doubt, the earth is His and He delegates the inheritance of it to whomsoever He pleases". (A'raf-128)

Now, since it is He Who delegates everything as pleases Him, its uses must also be according to His wishes. For man to use anything as a medium of tyranny is hateful to Him. Instead of blood sucking of one another, it is up to human beings to do good.

﴿وَٱبۡتَغِ فِيمَآ ءَاتَىٰكَ ٱللَّهُ ٱلدَّارَ ٱلۡأٓخِرَةَۖ وَلَا تَنسَ نَصِيبَكَ مِنَ ٱلدُّنۡيَاۖ وَأَحۡسِن كَمَآ أَحۡسَنَ ٱللَّهُ إِلَيۡكَۖ وَلَا تَبۡغِ ٱلۡفَسَادَ فِي ٱلۡأَرۡضِۖ إِنَّ ٱللَّهَ لَا يُحِبُّ ٱلۡمُفۡسِدِينَ ٧٧﴾
[القصص: 77]

"And whatsoever Allah has given you, use it as a doorway of the Hereafter. And do not forget whatever you have been given in this life, and just as Allah has been good to you, be you also good to others and do not make mischief in the land." (Qasas-77)

This implies that although Allah has allocated the "ownership" of things to individuals, the "ownership" is not uncharted, nor absolute, nor for disposal for one's own self-centred interests. It is bound by the commands of Allah. The individual may use it for his permissible benefit but not for encroaching on the rights of other individuals.

There are four basics of the defects of capitalism: bank interest, gambling, speculation, and hoarding. On the one hand, exploiting these four, the capitalist accumulates as much of the nation's wealth as he can, and on the other, he is not bound to dispose of his wealth on the poverty-stricken, the needy, the sick or the destitute. Charity is left to personal option.

Islam fastens the door against illegitimate means of earning income. Declaring interest, speculation, hoarding and gambling as the worst crimes, it announces:

﴿يَٰٓأَيُّهَا ٱلَّذِينَ ءَامَنُواْ لَا تَأۡكُلُوٓاْ أَمۡوَٰلَكُم بَيۡنَكُم بِٱلۡبَٰطِلِ إِلَّآ أَن تَكُونَ تِجَٰرَةً عَن تَرَاضٖ مِّنكُمۡۚ﴾ [النساء: 29]

"O you who believe! Do not devour the wealth of one another in falsehood, save in mutual agreement by way of trade". (Al Nisa-29)

"Interest" means that if the tradesman suffers a loss, the loss of the borrowed money is entirely his, the lender is not concerned in the least; and should the borrower make large profits, the profits too are all his and the lender does not partake of them in the least. In this way the wealth is concentrated instead of expanding and cannot circulate evenly. Instead, Islam proposes partnership (*shirkat*) and Mudarbah, so that both, borrower and lender, suffer in case of loss or profit.

Gambling and speculation, too, result in the concentration of wealth and normal circulation of it is hampered. Islam forbids all such means of income.

Besides imposing restrictions on all manners of forbidden of earning wealth, it makes a number of donations means compulsory, such as zakat of a fixed proportion of the savings and other items of expenditure for the public welfare. These items are not charity but leviable by legal force as compulsory. *Ushr* (tax of one-tenth on agricultural produce), *khiraj* (tribute), *sadqa e fitr* (Eid day charity), qurbani (sacrificing of animals), *kuffarah* (penitence money), *nufqaat* (maintenance allowances), *wasiyat* (will left by the deceased) and *wurasat* (laws of inheritance), are like streams flowing in various directions from a lake watering all the land around.

Alongwith these legal requirements, Islam develops a certain kind of mind. Instead of miserliness, hard-heartedness, selfishness, and lack of compassion, there arise sympathy, moral courage, large-heartedness, magnanimity, and, above all, fear of God. It is not possible for a Muslim to stop short at contenting himself with mere compliance of duties and shut his eyes towards the sufferings of fellow creatures. Every step of the way he is taught that this world is, but a transient garden and joy and happiness are the names not of hoards of gold and silver but of that peace and conscience which come on seeing the smile of a brother in well-being and which cause a garden to blossom forth in the life hereafter.

﴿وَيَسْـَٔلُونَكَ مَاذَا يُنفِقُونَ قُلِ ٱلْعَفْوَ﴾ [البقرة: 219]

"They ask you what they should spend, say, all that is above your basic needs. (Baqarah-219)

In short, by doing away with the impermissible items of income and increasing the expenditure items, the flow of wealth is directed towards society in general. It is a pity that in today's world these principles exist only in theory and a social economic order based on them is found implemented nowhere in the world. But go back in Muslim history to the early period when people went around looking for someone to give charity to but could find no one in need of it.

What can it be but a curse for our misdeeds that first we built our economic structure on capitalist principles; then, on seeing its harmful consequences, we begin clamouring for socialism and communism. In the first instance, tampering with the Quran and Traditions was done to legitimize the worst features of capitalism, namely, speculation and interest etc. and now socialism is being Islamised by distorting interpretations of the Quran and Traditions! It is high time we rid ourselves of our slavery to western modes of thinking and adopt seriously thought of Islamic principles to resolve our economic difficulties.

We appeal to those who look upon either of the two, capitalism or socialism as the road to salvation that instead of gluing patches of Islam onto a non-Islamic fabric, they should reflect on Islam. It is up to every citizen of a sovereign, free Islamic state not only to present himself as a true Muslim, but also invite others over the world to come out of the maze in which they are lost and take the path, the only path to success and happiness, which the Prophet Muhammed showed to the mankind fourteen centuries ago.

Economic improvements required for an Islamic Order[1]

What is the economic order of Islam as opposed to both capitalism and socialism?

This is the question most discussed today. How does this order, which professes to guarantee the well-being of all humanity, resolves a country's economic problems?

It should be made clear in the very beginning that the economic order of Islam is not a mere theoretic philosophy which the world has never seen in practice; it prevailed for several hundreds of years and, where it did, its blessings were witnessed by all and sundry and even the phrase 'economic injustices' ceased to be known. There was no distinction between the capitalist and the worker. All were members of one fraternity, helping one another in mutual sympathy; labour and peasantry were not held in disdain; they were respected as any other profession was; there was no monopoly over industry and trade to concentrate wealth in the hands of the big capitalists. All those doors were closed, which permitted the "big ones" to control the prices of consumer goods to break the poor man's backbone and subject him to an artificial famine!

This socio-economic order is not one that has been handed down generation after generation by mere word of mouth. Its details are to be found in black and white in a great many books. A sizeable part of Muslim Law, fiqah, is devoted to the Laws of Social Economics, and some authorities have included several of these laws in their legal jurisprudence.

---

[1] This paper is by Mufti Muhammed Shafi Sahab, my father. It was first published as an editorial in al-Balagh and, later, as a booklet. Still later, the proposals it contains were submitted by 18 ulema to the Government.

But it cannot be helped if Muslims refuse to spare a little time for studying their own religion and read the Quran and Traditions with a serious mind. When they hear the words 'Economic Order of Islam', they think that it is a novel term which has no thought, and which never had any factual existence anywhere. Hence the question, 'what is this economic order of Islam which the ulema say is better than both capitalism and socialism?

A detailed answer to the question would be to read the several books on the subject, but because the question is not purely theoretic to be read at leisure but is born of the urgent requirements of the time, an answer to which must be provided immediately, we shall present here some salient features to enable us to decide on the basic changes we shall have to make in our present structure; what will be the effect on the current system of wealth distribution and how an atmosphere of general prosperity can be created to everyone's benefit.

Our most pressing need concerns the injustice of the present system of wealth-distribution. The public is perfectly justified in complaining that only a few families are benefiting from the national economic progress, while the common man merely subsists on the verge of starvation. Today, Socialism is being presented to the capitalist persecuted world as an alternative, but the truth is that Islam and only Islam is the prescription for our ailments.

Reflecting deeply on the subject, we observe that the common man's economic affliction is due to pettiness of his income and of prevailing high prices. The responsibility for both rests on our capitalist economy, which concentrates the national wealth for the benefit of the few. If the Islamic economic order is implemented, both the basic causes would automatically be eliminated. We propose that:

1. The industrial monopolies existing in the form of cartels etc., should be declared illegal, and instead, an atmosphere of free

competition should be created so that impermissible profit-making may be minimized. Presently, because of the various industrial monopolies, the market is wholly in the hands of the big industrialists who manipulate prices by tampering with their natural fluidity. If these monopolies were eliminated, the surplus wealth that is channelled to their account would be diverted to the common man's benefit.

2. Key industries, such as railways, shipping, shipbuilding, steel, oil, etc., should be under state management, and their share should be allotted only to those whose monthly income is less than one thousand rupees, or whose bank balance is less than five-thousand rupees. The shares of those shareholders, whose income or bank balance is more than these amounts, should be forfeited.

   This method will be more beneficial than nationalizing, because nationalization does not divert the national wealth towards the needy, but installs the bureaucracy over it. The proposal submitted here directly makes the poor owners of the industries, and, as such, the capitalist or the government would not dominate them.

3. Bank-interest is the most formidable cause of wealth concentration. The profits that a bank derives from the collected deposits of the public go to the big capitalists who run their businesses on money borrowed from the banks, very little amount ultimately finds its way to the "public." For instance, hundreds of thousands of bales of cotton arrive in Karachi and are purchased by the few traders who have the bank's backing. No one invests his own money in this trade.

   In the Islamic social structure, this system will be wound up and, instead of running transactions, banking will be established on the principles of partnership and Mudarbah. The depositors would then share the bank's profits. This would result in eliminating the domination of the market by a few, leading to a reduction of prices, and there would be many co-sharers in the bank profits accruing proportionately from big business, hence national wealth will be circulating wider and wider.

What will be the practical way of running banks on principles of partnership and Mudarbah? Details have been published time and again and banking authorities have declared them to be perfectly practicable and also more beneficial.

(We shall soon be bringing out an outline draft on the subject).

4. The second cause of wealth concentration and dearness is blind speculation. A comprehensive work on this subject would be too voluminous. One example is that a commodity does not arrive in the market but several transactions of it already take place. One trader sells the commodity to another even before it is shipped; the latter sells it to another, and he, in turn, to yet another, and so on. By the time it arrives in the market, it has already been bought and sold many times. What wonder then if its price now is four or five times more than what it would otherwise have been. The speculators reap all the profits while the common man's purse gets thinner and thinner!

   Islam does not permit "blind transactions" at all. A commodity must be in the seller's possession when it is being sold. Speculation too will be done away with the advent of the Islamic economic order, resulting in the price reduction and the surplus profit which now goes into the hands of a few capitalists will benefit masses.

5. The third cause of wealth concentration is gambling. The entire system of insurance in based on gambling. The entire horse-racing, puzzle solving, lotteries and season tickets of games are different forms of gambling. Their victim is poor whose money is directed to one person. These forms of gambling will be forbidden under an Islamic government and making a fool of the public will not be permitted.

In the present insurance system the money belonging to the poor is drained out to the big capitalists who receive huge amounts of money on the excuse of this or that accident. The poor get but few chances of deriving any benefit from it. This means that the burden of the losses suffered by the big capitalists is also borne by the poor.

The insurance system will be replaced by mutual cooperative societies which will be free from gambling and interest-bearing transactions, allowing the poor to benefit more.

6. Hoarding and black-marketing will be punishable crimes and hoarders will be compelled to bring their hoarded commodities into the open market.
7. The license and permit system also contributes to the forming of monopolies. Bribes and favouritism secure the permits to the big capitalist. This too helps prices to spiral up and closes the door on those with small capital to enter market. On trade being freed of such practices, prices take downward trend, and an ordinary man too is enabled to enter business and industry. Today's labourer can become a factory owner tomorrow.
8. The present schedule of salaries is unfair, and the gaps between the grades are too wide. The differences will be reduced to the minimum.
9. Labor wages are on a very low level. In West Pakistan, the expenses per head of an average family of five is Rs. 220.00; in East Pakistan, Rs.260.00, but the wages are far below. In the different regions of Pakistan and different industries, the minimum wages have ranged from Rs.72.00 to Rs.117.00. The new labor policy fixes the maximum at Rs.140.00, but in the face of the ever-increasing prices, the increase in wages is still very unsatisfactory. To be realistic, a further increase is called for. An Islamic government

has the right to fix a minimum that is fairing to labor as well as practicable for the industrial structure.

There should be a labor wages board, comprising representatives of the government, labor and industrialist, to review the market from time to time and fix the minimum wages. It will be left to the bargaining capacity of labor to settle on wages above the minimum.

10. Government may also stipulate that labor shall be paid, in addition to its wages, special bonuses, overtime allowances or rewards for work done specially well, or, in lieu of the cash bonus they be given shares in some factory.

    It must be made clear that such increase in emoluments can prove meaningful only if, together with dissolving industrial monopolies, the conditions outlined above are also fulfilled. Otherwise, the increased labor income will only cause prices to rise and the money going to labor will be taken back by capitalist and the labor continuing in the same condition as before.

11. Like fixing of minimum wages for labor, an Islamic government has the right to stipulate the minimum of the peasant's share in *batai* transactions i.e., equitable division of crops between landlord and peasant. Here also, a board comprising government representatives, peasant and landlord may be set up for the purpose.
12. The *batai* system, also known as mazar-e-at, is not so bad, but the conditions, which the landlord imposes upon the peasant are absolutely invalid and, therefore, impermissible. And many of the conditions amount to forced labor. Stipulating any such conditions shall have to be made illegal.
13. If this matter cannot be controlled immediately, an Islamic government has the right also to declare that, for a transitory period, land shall be given out on contract and not on *batai*. Or that

the peasant shall work as a paid laborer receiving his remuneration as fixed by the government. Landlords may also be compelled, for a transitory period, to give a part of their land to a peasant in lieu of annual wages.

14. Laws shall be made to regulate the bringing of "barren land to life", as commanded by the shariah. That is, peasants who cultivate barren, un-owned land shall become its owners. Land given to a landlord for cultivation but who rented it out to a peasant shall be taken away from him and the peasant he declared its owner. The landlord shall also be compelled to return to such a peasant that part of the land produce which he might have taken from the peasant concerned.
15. All interest-bearing transactions involving land as security for loans shall be declared null and void. Lands already so burdened shall be returned to their lawful owners. The profits or whatever received by the lender shall be deducted from the amount lent, and if the profits exceed the loan, the excess shall be taken back and returned to the borrower.
16. In our country, accumulation of large areas of land in the ownership of one landlord is rampant due to the fact that the Islamic law of inheritance has not been followed up for a long time. A board shall be appointed to investigate such cases and have the lands distributed among the rightful co-sharers. If the Islamic inheritance laws are followed up there can never be large areas of land concentrated in the hands of one landlord.
17. Rules for easy transfer of lands should be drawn up and purchase and sale should be encouraged.
18. Government should provide interest-free soft loans to the peasants.
19. Agricultural implements and machinery should be made available to peasants who should also be properly trained for using them.

20. A cooperative organization should be set up to provide fertilizers, seeds and agricultural implements to peasants.
21. In our society agricultural produce goes through many stages, adding to the price at every stage. On the one hand, brokers and other middlemen deprive the cultivator of his due returns and, on the other, cause the market price to increase. This is why Islam abhors middle men in business transactions. Under the Islamic economic order, a number of organized markets will be set up where cultivator will sell directly to the consumer. As an alternative, cultivator-cooperatives may be organized for disposing the produce so that the huge sums of money now going to the middlemen may reach the cultivator.
22. Maintenance allowances and like will be only according to Islamic principles and given legal enforcement so that, besides the wife and children, near and distant relatives, and, in particular, orphans and widows, the sick and disabled, looking after whom the rich are advised, may enjoy legal security.
23. Supervision of zakat should be under a permanent department which should do the following acts:

    To collect arrears of zakat from all those on whom it has been due since the inception of Pakistan, and distribute it among the poor; Similarly, to collect zakat on animals and dispose of it in the same manner.

    Ushr and zakat on gold and silver will have to be paid by the owners but the Zakat Department will determine whether the payment is being made or not.
24. To provide employment to the unemployed is the government's responsibility. Unemployment allowances must be given to those whom the government cannot provide employment in spite of the best of its efforts.

25. The government should establish a 'Welfare Fund' from its annual budget to which donations may also be contributed. Industries may also be set up from this Fund to increase its assets. Houses should be constructed for the poor, and for laborers and peasants; a sufficient number of hospitals and free education up to matriculation should be provided; and other steps be taken for general welfare.
26. Abundance of money alone cannot improve a nation's condition. The people must abstain from wanton expenditure, especially on such items as encourage depravity. Wasting one's own money is undesirable but to waste the public money is a great crime. In our country, the greatest waste is the public treasury. Every year, huge amounts are spent on banquets, entertainment, official tours, travel abroad, government buildings' decorations and like. It will not be possible to put an end to all such waste, but it is forbidden in Islam and, therefore, a limit will have to be imposed on such expenditure and be strictly enforced. The moneys thus saved will be diverted to the national Welfare Fund.
27. A great amount of the national revenue is being spent on items entirely forbidden by Islam, for instance, import of liquor and films. These will be completely banned, and the foreign exchange thus saved will be diverted to the Welfare Fund. Non-Muslims may use liquor but must not import it.
28. Family Planning has done a great deal of harm to our economy. In the 3rd Five-Year Plan Rs. 284 million have been allocated to it while only Rs. 135 million to social welfare. It stands proved that Family Planning is un-Islamic, and being also socially and economically detrimental, it is unacceptable to the masses. The moneys spent on such planning should be diverted to peasant reform and increasing agricultural produce.

Administrative Reform:

In addition to the reforms stated above, large-scale changes are required in our administrative structure, which is one of the main causes of exploitation in our society. Our laws are perfectly sound in respect of many subjects, and justice is obtainable from them, but only if properly executed. Our administrative system is so full of flaws, so lethargic, lax, and undisciplined that justice remains no more than an embellishment of the books. When such is the condition of the administration, no law, however flawless, can do any good. Therefore, to make justice effective for social reform, it is necessary that the administration is made strong and dynamic.

Only the experts on administration can tell what the defects in our present social set-up are. For our social reconstruction, their services will be required. Here we can quote only some of the defects that are before our eyes.

Corruption:

Bribery is a crime impermissible, probably, in every society. Our Islamic law forbids it altogether, but in our country, it is committed freely and quite openly. It is rampant from the lowest police constable to the highest officers. He who can afford it may commit any number of crimes and get away with it, but he who cannot be innocent, yet finds no justice for himself. Such a state of affairs can be cured only by the honest and strong administrative officers. This can be done if the highest of them are given exemplary physical punishment and the law is made equally severe for all.

Justice:

Our judicial system is so old, complicated, painful and difficult that a poor man finds it more convenient to be patient about the wrong done to him than to vindicate his right. The law, civil and criminal, requires to be overhauled completely, and this may take time, but certain steps should be taken immediately.

For deciding industrial disputes there should be special courts easily accessible for the workers.

Summary courts be established for deciding disputes between landlords and peasants and for relieving the peasants of the burden of tyrannical agreements imposed on them.

For relieving women of their persecution, there should be mobile courts empowered to decided cases without unnecessary delay.

Labor:

There are enough laws, including the Factories Act, for the benefit of the health of workers, protection against accidents, against excessive work, salaries, etc., but none of them is respected. Under the Factories Act, proper ventilation, light, sanitation, protection against the weather are stipulated as necessary and inspectors are appointed to keep an eye on them, but what is really done is that the factory owners pay the inspector a monthly "allowance" to overlook everything that may be wrong. For the show of it, the inspector sends up a few ordinary chalans now and then in a year and deposits nominal amount of the fine in the government treasury. Labor is not benefited by the law at all. Its place of work is too cold in winter and too hot in summer for work; unhealthy food is sold in the canteens; the latrines are too dirt-laden for words. When such are the conditions, no law, however good, can be effective.

Red Tape:

There is too much of it in our offices, as anyone who has anything to do with them knows. On the one hand, those people who do not have the right approach find no easy way of redress; and, on the other, work between department and department and, office and office is delayed, file upon file piles up, money is wasted, and no job comes to the finishing line.

These few examples of the great defects of our administrative system are given hereby because they affect our social economy. Unless improvements in the law as well as in the working of the administration are made, the public will not be relieved of its difficulties.

Need for Simple Living:

Another important cause of the sufferings of the people is Western culture, which we have adopted. Islam commands simple living even though gold and silver rain on us from the skies. If an Islamic social order is to be implemented here, we shall have completely to reform our personal lives.

a) We shall have to give up luxury and expensive ways which we have imported from the West because of which the masses are suffering so much. Our condition today is that we blindly follow the western pattern of dress, the western style of holding functions, in short, the western way of life in everything and look upon this blind copying as a sign of being civilized. No one is looked upon as cultured and civilized unless he wears an expensive western style suit, lives in a bungalow with most up-to-date trimmings, such as, refrigerators, TV, and expensive furniture. If such articles are to be symbols of high culture, why will everyone not try to outstrip another in possessing them, and, to that end, when the resources are meagre, why should recourse not be made to bribes, smuggling, robbery and such other criminal ways.

   To change all this, it will be necessary for the cabinet ministers, high officers, political leaders, and social workers to start a movement for adopting simplicity in all spheres of life. To do so they will have to begin with themselves. Until such simplicity is achieved, the masses will not be relieved of the artificiality, which is the cause of their plight, and the consequences of which for a poor country like Pakistan can only be ruinous.

b) Import of luxury goods must be banned and indigenous industries for the manufacture of consumer goods should be encouraged.

c) Import of such consumer goods should also be banned as are already being manufactured of equal or better quality in the country; clothe for example. This will contribute to savings in foreign exchange and also to simplicity in life.

d) A maximum limit, legally enforceable, should be placed on expenses incurred on marriages and other functions.

e) There are some trades and industries, which are socially injurious, but it seems impossible to get rid of them. This is why people who recognize them to be bad, hesitate to advise their closure. But, if we are to be realistic, we shall have to act with courage, however, strange this may appear at first.

   The film industry and television, for instance, are two evils which have brought the nation to the very lowest end of immorality. They have done nothing but harm. How can it be justifiable for people of whom ninety per cent are illiterate, live on the verge of starvation and quite unfamiliar with the sciences and technology, to spend millions and millions on shows and sport that are proving a veritable poison for the nation's health, clean thinking and general ethics. It is like setting fire to one's own house to enjoy it as a show!

   It would contribute towards economic progress if the same money were invested in constructive industries. Islam looks upon healthy entertainment as something good, but not one that is detrimental to health, morals and financial well-being.

f) In our society, status is based on profession but such norms are un-Islamic and are borrowed from non-Muslims. It is opposed to the

Islamic concept of equality and obstructs the free mobility of labor without which a balanced natural economy is impossible. This defect in our social fabric can be removed only by proper education, the public media and launching movements to that end.

g) It is very necessary to elevate the social status of labor, peasants and the servant class. According to Islam, the employer and the employee are but two individuals of the same fraternity and on the same level of social status. Therefore, there is no reason why the employer should look down upon his employee as someone below him and treat him as an unequal. On a breach of agreement either of the two has the same right to demand satisfaction of the other. It is not proper that the employee should be bound to treat his employer with all due respect while the employer treats him with disdain. Here, too, the right education and assistance of the public media are required to change the individual's and social mentality. Laws should also be framed to punish employers for contemptuous treatment of their employees. This will assist social and moral reform and also contribute to simple living.

Finally, we should like to draw the reader's attention to a basic point. It is no secret that tyranny and exploitation are the product of that diseased mind which is not concerned with the fear of God, the life Hereafter, or morality. The evils found in our society are due to self-centredness, hard-heartedness, and lack of generosity, helped by our contact with the materialist West. If the Islamic social order were implemented, and because Islam is based on the fear of God and faith in the Hereafter, hearts and minds would be reconstructed, laws changed, education and public media run on different channels, all geared as one movement.

Experience throughout the world shows that the law by itself achieves nothing to reform a nation or put an end to persecution and exploitation, unless backed by strong spiritual faith. During the first period of Islam, the instances we find of self-sacrifice, sympathy, spending in the path of God, generosity and non-attachment, are due to the fear of God and concern for the hereafter, which were buried deep in the very core of the hearts and minds of the believers. If the same emotions and zeal could be revived today, we should enjoy the times of Omar bin Abdul Aziz once again!

This revolution of the soul and mind may appear impossible to some people, but if government should make this revolution its ideal and work for it on the right lines, success is bound to come within a very short time, transforming the fortunes of this country. However bad we may be today, there is yet a spark of faith left somewhere beneath and, if someone blows on it, it is bound to blaze forth into a raging fire!

After all, this nation is the same that gave proof of extraordinary deeds twice in its history: first, during the partition in 1947 and the other, in 1965. On both occasions it acted with such courage, discipline, spirit of sacrifice, fellow-sympathy and generosity which amazed the world. Is it not the same nation that today we are shedding tears over for its selfishness, lack of discipline, miserliness and general corruption?

The more we think of it the more are we convinced that at that time the national leaders had set the spark ablaze and the public realized that they were being called upon in the name of Islam for real righteous work. But today, there is none to kindle the spark into a fire again. If only someone would rise to do it and call upon the nation to response with sacrifices, the nation would, in a very short time become incomparable. If a people can perform deeds during war reminiscent of Yarmook and Qadisyah, why cannot it do things during peace to resurrect the times of Omar bin Abdul Aziz.

It is necessary.

To make the education system purely Islamic and conduct the bringing up of the students along Islamic lines.

That the administrators should give up their western style of life and set an example of renunciation and sacrifice before the access.

That the public media, including radio and newspapers be run on Islamic lines. Immodesty, indecency in all its forms, love of comfortable ease should be replaced with such programs as encourage national pride, collective thinking, the spirit of sacrifice, fear of God and concern for the Hereafter.

That knowledge of Islamic requirements be made compulsory and included among the qualifications of administrative officers. A vigilant eye should be kept on character, and character, not degrees, should be considered for application.

That there be a permanent government department for enforcing "what is commanded" and "restraining from what is forbidden". (*Amr e bil maaroof and nahi anil munkir*). This department will consist of God-fearing, practicing Muslims devoted entirely to creating the spirit of Islam among the masses.

That mosque, the centres of an Islamic society, be used as such. High government officers should launch a movement for "establishing *sallat*", *aqamat e sallat*, and for the purpose, begin with themselves.

If these proposals are acted upon by the government, a nation can be built up here that will be an envy for the whole world in respect of its character, thoughts, emotions, deeds and performance. The world will then see how peaceful, just and satisfactory the socioeconomics of the country can be under Islam as opposed to the other which are full of tensions and anxieties.

Difficulties always beset every important task, especially one that is revolutionary. But it should also be remembered that no revolution can be launched in Pakistan so easily as the Islamic one. First, the proposals submitted in these pages are not too difficult to implement. Second, the Pakistani soil is better suited to Islam than any other in the world. The most effective power to make a revolution successful is the nation's fervour and emotions of which there is no want among our peoples. Love for Islam and the desire to see it rise to the pinnacle of honour are steeped in their blood. If they see that efforts are really being made here to bring about an Islamic revolution, they will go through the most demanding of trials for its sake.

On the other hand, if any effort is made here for a socialist movement, there will be so many difficulties in the way that there will be no peace for years and years. Socialist history shows that bloodshed, force, violence and turmoil are indispensable to it. Besides, socialism is not desired by the people. It cannot be implemented but forced. The masses will never heartily work for it and a tug of war between them, and the government will go on for centuries.

Besides socialism cannot put an end to socio-economic disequilibrium. Nationalizing land and factories will not end the poor man's difficulties but increase them. The protagonists of socialism have ambiguous slogans to shout about but no precise, organized and thought-provoking program to offer.

The Ulema Plan

An agreed socio-economic plan of 118 ulema and spreading over 22 Points, has been published recently. It bears the signatures of ulema from all the different schools of thought. The Plan is undoubtedly a great achievement for them and it is hoped, these 22 Points, like the 22 Points of the Constitution of 1952, will prove to be a milestone in the history of the fight for the implementation of Islamic values.

The question asked quite vociferously everywhere was:

> *What exactly is that Islamic economic order which is being talked about as superior to both socialism and capitalism for mankind's welfare, and how is it to be implemented?*

The Plan submitted by the ulema is an answer to the two parts of this question. The basics of Islamic economics are clearly stated. Anyone who reads them with due care will appreciate that to relieve Muslims of the tyranny of capitalism and its exploitation of the masses, one does not have to turn to Moscow or Peking.

It is a very significant and encouraging aspect of this Plan that the ulema of ever sect and thought have contributed to it: Sunni. Shiaite, Ahle Hadith, Deobandi and Barelvi, all are represented here. It was long believed that there was no unity among the Muslim ulema and, therefore, such a thing as an Islamic socio-economic order was not possible.

But the truth is that the differences among the ulema are in respect only of the ceremonials of worship or trivial matter and none over such as concern the collective values or may obstruct the implementation of Islamic socioeconomics. As far as state constitution is concerned, there is not a single difference among the sects. In 1951, a convention of the notable ulema was held where 22 Points were agreed upon, Over the years no one has raised any objection to them, and, indeed, it has been urged time and again by religious leaders everywhere that our constitution should be based on these 22 points. Similarly, there is no difference of opinion worth mentioning about the "personal laws" which the 22 points lead entirely to the sect concerned. There been no difference on such a vital subject, the services of the ulema has have been highly appreciated throughout the country, including the experts on economics, besides, of course, political leaders and journalists. Economists have said that if these Points were factually implemented, an atmosphere of general welfare would certainly emerge.

We may now dilate on the effects of the Plan under consideration.

There are two angles from which a socio-economic Plan, unanimously agreed upon, should be considered. Firstly, how far are the basic points consistent with Islam? And, secondly, how far are they practicable in the present times?

As far the first, it is sufficient that the ulema of every religious school of thought, who have the confidence of the whole ummah, are agreed upon them. A special feature of these proposals is that they are purely Islamic, and no non-Islamic patches have been foisted on them.

Because Islam gives a perfect code of life, good for all ages and all times, it does not have to be changed according to the varying times. In itself it is resilient enough to cope with their demands. Those of its commands, which are of permanent value, concern matters, which cannot affect them. For problems, which may be influenced by the changing times, Islam lays down rules and principles, which may be modified so as to show the right way. There are yet other counsels and commands to deal with situations arising out of emergencies.

This is the point at which it becomes difficult to distinguish between investigation of truth and mere tampering. That is why only those people can do it who have spent their lives in the study of the Quran and sunnah and ransacking the treasure of the shariah to understand the word and spirit of religion, Deen. The ulema who have drawn up the 22-point plan possess these qualifications. Every point, however, intricate or delicate, has been deliberated upon. Some of the proposals concern transitory problems, such as the fixing of prices by the government. The real objective of Islam is to eliminate all manner of monopolies from the market and replace them with free competition so that commodity prices and labour wages may adjust themselves. Economists agree that there is no other way to bring down prices to the lowest level.

No artificial permanent price control has ever succeeded in doing this. Eliminating monopolies cannot be done overnight and, therefore, Islam permits price control only for a transitory period.

Similarly, according to Islam, property earned by permissible means cannot be confiscated by the State and, therefore, the ulema have not made any such proposal in their Plan. But because of centuries of wrong socioeconomics, wealth has become concentrated in the hands of the few, leading to a great many enormities and evils. Therefore, the ulema have made several alternative proposals, which are according to Islam and also seek to put an end to wealth-concentration and replace it with a balanced economy. For instance:

In para 6 of the Plan, the proposal made is that in all semi-government owned industries shares should be sold only to those whose incomes are less than Rs.1,000/- per month. And the agreement made with those whose incomes are above this amount and who shares in such industries should be terminated at the end of the current year as per rules of the shariah. The proposal, in contrast with nationalising the key industries, will be more beneficial to the poor because nationalisation does not directly make the poor owners of them as the Plan intends to do by making them share the profits.

In para 19 of the Plan, it has been proposed that arrears of zakat payable by those industrialists who have not paid it should be realised from them and distributed among the poor.

Para 10 states that government should impose a condition on the industrialists to the effect that they should pay the workers for overtime or work done specially well, and such, special bonuses in the shape of shares in the industries instead of cash.

Para 14 proposes that to offset the concentration of land in a few hands, the Islamic law of inheritance should be strictly enforced. This will distribute land reducing the holdings to the minimum and among the many.

Para 11 proposes that because of the peasant-persecution involved in the batai or crop-sharing system, the government should, for a transitory period, make it obligatory for the landlord either to give his land out on contract for cultivation or give portions of his land to the cultivator in lieu of payment in cash or kind.

Para 13 recommends that all lands held as security for loans on interest should be released by the government and returned to the debtor, and the amount of the interest already paid to the lender should be debited from the amount of loan.

It cannot be doubted that if these proposals were implemented, the terrible imbalance of the economy this country is going through would be rectified and the ground cleared for Islamic socio-economic order to bear fruit.

These proposals concern the immediate steps required to be taken for eliminating the evils created by concentration of wealth under capitalism. The proposals made for establishing the economy on Islamic foundations are revolutionary and, therefore, very important.

The first of the subsequent proposals seeks to eliminate interest. There is no reason for denying that "interest" has done the greatest harm to our system of wealth-distribution. It is that curse which has impoverished the overwhelming masses only to foster a few big capitalists. Interest-bearing transactions are like a syringe used for drawing out the blood of the masses. The ulema have proposed that banking and insurance companies should be cleansed of interest giving and taking and run on principles of co-sharing and Mudarbah so that the profits earned on the moneys deposited by the people may be proportionately distributed among them and not merely among the capitalists.

The method of running banks and insurance companies according to co-sharing and Mudarbah has been published several times by religious bodies and other intellectuals. Our economists and banking experts, too, have admitted repeatedly that this system is quite practical and more beneficial for the nation's general prosperity. The work is, of course, of a revolutionary nature and it will take time and considerable effort to make it yield the desired results, but it has to be done to put right the wrong we ourselves have committed.

Those of our compatriots, who have enslaved their vision to the West, create considerable confusion by holding that if "interest" were eliminated from banking, business transactions with foreign countries would become impossible. True, it is beyond our power to eliminate "interest" throughout the world; we shall have to do it first in our own country. If we cannot relieve the whole world of an epidemic, it does not mean that we should not relieve ourselves of it!

An Islamic state should first put matters aright in itself, eliminate banking-interest here display a pattern for all Muslim countries to follow, and establish trade ties mostly with them as it will be easier for them to establish their economy on interest-free basis. As for non-Muslim countries trade with whom is indispensable, effort should be made to conduct it on the barter system (which is already being done between the socialist and capitalist countries); and if there is no alternative but to accept their terms, it may be done on the principle of Islam which relaxes its principles when confronted with compulsions.

Also, if the Muslim countries really make up their minds with self-confidence, to get rid of "interest", they will soon be in a position to make the world agree to their conditions. Their pattern of economy can also show them the light to adopt it for themselves; and, at least, the non-Muslim countries can be compelled to conduct their transactions with Muslim countries on principles of interest-free banking. But this can be accomplished only with zeal and determination. The nations which permit difficulties to obstruct forward movement do not become live nations. Success is fated only for those who go through the most difficult of situations forging their path onward and onward.

The next evolutionary proposal made by the ulema is for the total banning of speculations, which is the main cause of the excessively high prices prevailing in the market today. Speculative trading enables a few avaricious ones to play with the economy of millions and millions of the masses. Because of this tyrannical game, a commodity does not come to the market before it goes through scores of transactions, so that by the time it arrives, its price has already rocketed ski high. For this reason, the Prophet forbade selling a commodity before it came into seller's possession. If this principle is followed strictly, the consumer would benefit from the profits the speculators now get away with.

In the working of the stock exchanges, it is speculation that causes economic upheavals in the market. Sometimes one single speculator can create an upheaval for the whole country and bring it to the verge of ruin. Moreover, speculation is developed as an art that involves hundreds of traders in dishonesty and fraud and other moral crimes. Many a scandal is fostered within the walls of stock exchange.

The third revolutionary proposal calls for putting an end to the current permit system of foreign trade. Restrictions on free trade result in the creation of monopolies. The whole nation has an equal right to its foreign exchange but, as things are, the masses get nothing but paper currency notes while the whole available foreign exchange is at the disposal of the big capitalists. The common man is so bound that he cannot import even with his own assets without buying foreign exchange from the government. This obliges the public to buy only from the big capitalists, and these capitalists sell articles of inferior quality at exorbitant prices. They hold the market monopoly, and the public's money pours into their pockets.

If this proposal for free trade is accepted, the monopolies would break up, small businessmen would come up, there would be free competition, and commodities would be available to the masses at cheap prices. Wealth would circulate over a wider spectrum affecting the whole economy for the better.

The fourth revolutionary proposal is that cartels and similar monopolies should be banned. Some capitalists get together to fix a price for a certain commodity, thus denying the benefits of free enterprise to the masses. Any such agreement that causes a price hike is forbidden in Islam.

The fifth revolutionary proposal seeks to eliminate middlemen from the trade of agricultural products. This should be done by mutual cooperatives of the peasants so that they may receive proper remuneration for their labour and prices may be kept low because of the elimination of middlemen. To derive the full benefits, these cooperatives should be based on small areas so that an atmosphere of free trade may prevail in the grain market and prices may not rise high.

To save the peasant from persecution, the ulema have proposed certain methods to improve the crop-sharing system. Proposals have also been made to enable the peasant to become owner of the land he cultivates.

It is not our purpose here to enumerate all the proposals made by the ulema. Only some proposals and their effects have been mentioned in these pages to show that the ulema have seriously reflected on them from a thoroughly practical angle, ignoring the present slogan mongering of the day. For instance, great stress is being laid on wage increase, but we decided to lay greater stress on price reduction. If wages are increased, say, twofold but prices increase three times, labour's conditions remain the same. The common man's problem, more than less income, is that of high expenditure. No step taken towards improving his condition can be of benefit to him until the problem of dearness is resolved. The ulema have kept this basic point in mind throughout their work.

Most of our difficulties have been created by none but ourselves. We have made our lives artificial, and luxury ridden far beyond our economic capacity. The ulema are thoroughly right that unless simple living is adopted and a forceful movement launched to that end, and government officials and the wealthy make a beginning with themselves, there will be no general prosperity. We weep our misery, yet we have made pleasure-loving habits inseparable from our lives. This virtually is to enjoy seeing our own house on fire. Improvement without renouncing luxury is not possible.

Implementation of these proposals will, no doubt, take time and labour without which no revolution can be effected. But it can be said with confidence that in our country no revolution can be brought about with less difficulty than the Islamic, the reason for which is that we possess the Shariah as well as Islamic enthusiasm and fervour which inspire and incline us to make the greatest of sacrifices. But this is conditional: the motive will have to be not merely to profess the name of Islam but to implement Islam with a sincere heart.

Allah be thanked that our people, in spite of their many weaknesses, still want to live as Muslims and die as Muslims, and are prepared to sacrifice for Islam, proof of which the world saw with its own eyes in 1947 and again in 1965. Should the country ever turn towards true Islam, the world will see once again how amazing a capacity we have for absorbing Islam.

On the other hand, if, God forbid, socialism comes here, irrespective of whether it is beneficial or harmful, it will be extremely difficult to implement; at every step, Islam will obstruct its path, and the people will never genuinely accept it in their hearts.

It is now necessary to move forward in the light of this unanimously agreed plan of the ulema. In our opinion, all those political parties which desire an Islamic social order should include the plan in their manifestos.

Our Economic Problems and Islamic proposals for resolving them.[2]

As opposed to socialism, the economic plan being submitted by the ulema is in the category of ijtihad, juristic, who can know better than the ulema that if expression of differences is not permitted, what is right and what is wrong in law cannot be determined. It would be equal to depriving the ummah of a great blessing. How great a deprivation it is, should be known best by a nation that has just emerged from ten years of Ayub's dictatorship.

The masses are never the addressees of juristic arguments, but it would be quite gratifying if, together with economic programmes published in various journals, the principles of juristic debate were also included with commentary and appropriate detail. Inquiry about some principles well not be out of place.

Among Western thinkers, the famous historian Arnold Toynbee has a distinguished status. He writes that in today's world, the great cause of its sufferings are the fact that science and technology and nationalism and patriotism are opposed to one another. Science expands man's horizons while patriotism restricts and reduces them; science moves forward to universalize for the better, patriotism frustrates the blessings of science. In Europe when the industrial revolution took place, emotions of patriotism also rose high. This coincidence brought with it the curse of colonialism and imperialism. Today the depressed nations of the east called, developing nations, borrow science and technology from the West

---

[2] This essay by Dr. Syed Muhammad Yusuf is a discussion on the country's basic economic problems, and includes points raised now and again by the ulema. At the end, we have stated our opinion on the subject in some detail.

by the method of copying-according-to-the-original, together with Our Economic Problems & Proposals for Resolving Them nationalism and chauvinism, and, therefore, the masses get over- burdened in the name of patriotism and whatever progress industry makes the wealth of it concentrates in the hands of the few.

Now, when such is the intolerable condition, it is being proposed that industries should be nationalized. Let us take an example. The natural result of technological advance should be that cotton cloth should be available to me at a very small price; and in the natural course, patriotism would also progress, and prices would go on decreasing. If this did not happen, the machine would never take the place of the handloom. Patriotism and nationalism upset these natural results and the cloth of a very poor quality manufactured in my own country is made available to me at a high price. Knowing well that such business is against human nature, I am persecuted. The import of cheaper and better cloth is banned. In short, technology offers me good and clean cloth at 50 paisa a meter but forced patriotism gives me the same cloth of poor quality at Rs. 3.00 a meter.

How are indigenous industries set up? Briefly, in order to export, we are made to starve, (we simply long for good quality rice and tea). Government takes possession of the foreign exchange earned from cotton, jute, rice and tea and palms on paper currency to us! To this foreign exchange are added those loans which are borrowed on interest from the developed countries. No loan is free of political strings attached to it.

Government transfers this foreign exchange to some industrialist, who sets up an industry, which now has the government's 'protection', encouragement and full support. This means that only goods manufactured in the country are sold, however rotten they might be. The burden of this falls on the average consumer. A part of the high price the customer has to pay is taken away by the government as tax and the rest goes to fatten the capitalist. The masses may not be expert economists, but their conclusions based on experience are always correct. It is well known to them that the goods manufactured in the country become increasingly expensive; their availability too is uncertain and there is always the danger of adulteration and fraud. It would not matter if things went only so far. Recently when Ayub required a donation, the industrialist created an artificial scarcity of his products and prices spiralled up. The dearness broke the worker's backbone while the capitalist went on exploiting him.

Government increases its indirect taxes and permits the capitalist to suck everybody's blood. The ever-increasing high prices add to mass poverty and labor's unspeakably miserable condition, but further augment the capitalist's capital. All this is the result of the 'protection' given in the name of patriotism.

When the capitalist's manipulations come up before the public's eye, the government resorts to the prescription advanced by none other than the authorities of the West; nationalization, which means diverting the money coming out of the consumer's pocket from the capitalist to the governments treasury to be spent on public welfare works, so that the public may benefit.

Things to be determined:

From the purely shariah angle, how is the government justified in banning imports in order to compel the consumer to purchase goods produced by one or a few countable capitalists at arbitrarily fixed prices and go on tolerating their artificial scarcity and ever-increasing prices?

Will this be permissible only in the same country? For instance, may some landlords of Sind ban the import of grain from the Punjab to sell their own produce at their own arbitrary prices?

Is there any comparable instance to be found in the times of the Holy Prophet or in His first four Caliph (the *Rashideen*)? How far does 'protection' accord with Islamic principles?[3]

The arguments so far advanced against nationalization are all based on reasoning the bureaucracy will dominate; standard of work will go down; it will not be better for labor, and so on.

If no shariah principle is opposed to it, differences of opinion must be tolerated. Why should nationalization conjure up thought of atheism? The ulema themselves are suggesting that some industries should be run by the government but keep away from the cloth industry. I am referring to the basics of the shariah, otherwise, there are volume upon volume of books for and against nationalisation.

Everyone is familiar with a Tradition, which is frequently quoted in the journals, but no one reflects on it, although it is of basic importance. I should like my opinion to be criticized, for or against.

---

[3] In today's world the method of setting up national industries of which a brief outline has been given above is looked upon as the sine qua non of progress. Anyone who opposes it in the least is looked upon as an opponent of progress. It is only the ulema who are not deterred by censure. Riba is also looked upon as essential to progress. Several ulema did show some weakness on this subject but the majority of them prevailed. However, 'protection' and price control they seem inclined to accept. Their premise is not the use or the media of use but the basic thought calls for critical inquiry. They upset the natural working of economic laws. Is this not against Islam? It was surprising to see Maulana Muhammed Idrees of Meerut look upon foreign loans as indispensable, (perhaps, even permissible. (Bainaat December 1969 p.21). Only one page after (p. 23), the Tradition:

لعن رسول الله آكل الربا ومؤكله

Allah's Prophet has cursed Riba etc. Perhaps the Maulana forgot. If loans on interest from foreign countries are held impermissible industrial progress will be deprived of one of its main supports.

Someone requested the Holy Prophet,

روى أنس قال: غلا السعر على عهد النبي ﷺ، فقالوا: يا رسول الله، لو سعرت لنا؟ فقال: إن الله هو القابض، الباسط، الرزاق، المسعر، وإني لأرجو أن ألقى الله وليس أحد منكم يطلبني بمظلَمة ظلمتُه إياه في دم ولا مال." رواه أبو داود والترمذي وصححه.

روى أبو داود وغيره حديث العلاء بن عبد الرحمن، عن أبيه، عن أبي هريرة رضي الله عنه فقال: "بل الله يرفع ويخفض، وإني لأرجو أن ألقى الله وليس لأحد عندي مظلمة".

In my opinion, Islam does not approve of the government assuming the responsibility of controlling rates and prices. This should not be done as far as possible. In other words, economic processes should be allowed to work unfettered and without government interference.

Ibn Qim al- Jauzia has discussed price control from various angles in his *al- Taraq ul Hikmiya fi Sayasat al- Shariah* (Egypt 1317 AH, p.223 and following). He supports the idea that where selfish elements come in التواطأ على الأغلاء [to negotiate debt], the government should make التقويم بقيمة المثل [calendar in the form of compulsory] so as to support the normal economic processes. The government does not fix prices of its own. *Qeemat ul misl* is that which fixes itself as a result of the interplay of economic laws in a free market. All the government does is unearth and identify, and protect against the manipulations of self-centered elements.

"Today, price control is taken to imply that the government puts an end to the normal working of economic laws and assumes the authority to fix wages and prices. This is necessitated by the fact that the government itself imposes restrictions on import and export, arbitrarily establishes industries, gives 'protection' on the excuse of patriotism, forces selected goods on the consumers, and fixes prices at its own sweet will. Prices are, in either case, arbitrary. That is why wages are auctioned, political parties offer higher and higher bids. Who can tell what the price level of food-grains will be after October 5, 1970? Or how the other normal economic processes will be affected? It is because of these industries that government assumes control of all trade or keeps it within its own imposed limits. The obnoxious license permit system is evidence of زاد الطين بلته.

In short, what the government does is not control prices but what makes price control necessary. This is downright mischief on the government's part, which is given the pseudonym of 'price control'.

Ibn Qeem al Jauzia has made an analysis of conditions prevailing in his time (middle of the 8th century) when price control might have been necessary. We may conclude that in that age there was no industry which required 'protection'. We find only one example which we may suspect: let us see what the consequence was:

ومن أقبح الظلم إيجار الحانوت على الطريق أو في القرية بأجرة معينة على أن لا يبيع أحد غيره، فهذا ظلم حرام على المؤجِّر والمستأجر، وهو نوع من أخذ أموال الناس قهرًا وأكلها بالباطل، وفاعله قد تحجَّر واسعًا، فيُخاف عليه أن يحجر الله عنه رحمته كما حجَّر على الناس فضله ورزقه.ص(224)

Do the rights being given to the government today not fall within the purview of نوع من أخذ أموال الناس قهرا and تحجر واسعا When the economist admits that cruelty and arbitrariness exist, he recommends price control so that the people's wealth may not pour into the capitalist's pockets, but the benefits may be re-diverted to the people via the government. (My purpose is not to support nationalization but to condemn price control).

It is also a fact that the system of price control is unending. It may be beneficial for short periods, but just as a good medicine loses its effect if used too long so does price control when continued too far. Today price control, *takhteet* and *laqmeen* are prevalent in the developed nations of the West, but no one has any peace of mind. Everyday things go out of control and there are large-scale economic upheavals and disorganization. The government must fix prices, the government must fix wages, the government must fix the division- ratio of crops between cultivator and peasant. This does not seem to be a satisfactory or long-lasting solution to economic ills.

Administration of agricultural land is a basic problem and requires careful deliberation because the mischief prevailing today is not brought about the capitalist alone but by his alliance with the feudalism. Without feudalism at its back, there would never have been such insensibility in capitalism. First, feudalism reduces the individual to a state of helplessness, then, taking advantage of his condition, the capitalist exploits him. This is what happened in Europe and is happening in our country. In a country like ours, no problem of labor, far less than that of the peasantry, can be resolved until land administration is established firmly on justice.

There are two schools of thoughts, both independent and both mutually contradictory:

One holds that unlimited ownership is thoroughly according to the shariah whether it be by *un tariq al sharaa* or *un tariq ul aqta*;

As a corollary to this right *mazare-at* is also justified, as Ibn Qeem al Jauzia writes:

قال شيخ الإسلام وغيره من الفقهاء: والمزارعة أحل من المتاجرة وأقرب إلى العدل، فإنهما يشتركان في المغرم والمغنم، بخلاف المآجرة، فإن صاحب الأرض يُسلّم له

الأجرة، والمستأجر قد يحصل له زرع وقد لا يحصل له زرع.

والعلماء مختلفون في جوازهما سواء كانت الأرض إقطاعًا أو غيره.

قال شيخ الإسلام ابن تيمية: وما علمت أحدًا من علماء الإسلام من الأئمة الأربعة ولا غيرهم قال: "إجارة الإقطاع لا تجوز"، وما زال المسلمون يؤجرون إقطاعاتهم قرنًا بعد قرن، من زمن الصحابة إلى زمننا هذا، حتى حدث بعض أهل زماننا فابتدع القول ببطلان إجارة الإقطاع. وولي الأمر يأذن للمُقطَع في الإجارة، فإنه إنما أقطعهم لينتفعوا بها، إما بالمزارعة وإما بالإجارة.

ومن منع الانتفاع بها بالإجارة والمزارعة، فقد أفسد على المسلمين دينهم ودنياهم، وألزم الجند والأمراء أن يكونوا هم الفلاحين، وفي ذلك من الفساد ما فيه.

The other school of thought holds *al mazaria* (*bashar o taha*) as permissible but *akra ul ard bil zahab wa al fizza* as not permissible.

Ibn Haz am writes:

إن النبي ﷺ قدم عليهم وهم يكرون مزارعهم، كما روى رافع وغيره، وقد كانت المزارع بلا شك تُكرى قبل رسول الله ﷺ وبعد مبعثه، هذا أمر لا يمكن أن يشك فيه ذو عقل. ثم صح من طريق جابر، وأبي هريرة، وأبي سعيد، ورافع ظهير البدري، وآخر من البدريين، وابن عمر: نهى رسول الله ﷺ عن كِراء الأرض، فبطلت الإباحة بيقين لا شك فيه.

فمن ادّعى أن المنسوخ (إباحة الكِراء) فقد رَجع، وإن تَعيُّن النسخ قد بَطَل، فهو كاذب مكذّب، قائل ما لا علم له به، وهذا حرام بنصّ القرآن، إلا أن يأتي على ذلك ببرهان، ولا سبيل إلى وجوده أبدًا، إلا في إعطائها بجزءٍ مسمّى مما يخرج منها،

(كالثُّلث والرُّبع)، فإنه قد صحّ أن رسول الله ﷺ فعل ذلك بخيبر بعد النهي بأعوام، وأنه بقي على ذلك إلى أن مات عليه السلام. (المحلّى)

One may not agree with Ibn Hazam but considering his learning, piety and sincerity, his position is not such that his words may not be heard with attention. If, today, someone holds such an opinion of him, it may be said that the man does not know enough or has misunderstood, but it does not follow that he is an atheist.[4]

This is only by way of digression. Both these schools are right whatever be rajah or marjooh, or whichever of the two be correct or incorrect, and whether the Tradition's link be weak or strong, it carries the same logic as the other.[5]

The feudalist's tyranny is an acknowledged fact. Truth can no longer be denied. The consequences of the thinking of the former school, about which we have so far been indifferent, are before us though they are inhuman, as commonly believed. Such being the facts, to continue with unconcern is no longer possible. Therefore, the "Islamic" seal has been

---

[4] This proposal is part of the manifesto of a political party. I do not know whether the ulema supported it or not.

[5] Atheism unimaginable In al Baas ul Islami Lucknow. Mahmud abuk I Saud writes in Adad Uliyu 1969.

الأرجح عندنا أن للفردان يملك الأرض الزراعية، وذلك لا شك استغلالٌ لرأس المال، ولكن ليس له قطعًا أن يُكريها. ولَعَمري، إن اشتراط كِراء الأرض نظيرَ مبلغٍ معينٍ من ذهب أو فضة، لهو أمعنُ في الخطأ، وأقمنُ بالحكم بالتحريم لا بالتحليل، وأبعدُ ما يكون عن منطق الإسلام، وجديرٌ أن لا يكون صادرًا عن رسول الله ﷺ. إذ كيف يأبى أن تُؤجَّر الأرض بجزءٍ مما يخرج منها، ثم يرى أن يدفع المستأجر لصاحبها حصةً معيَّنةً من ذهب أو فضة؟!

affixed to curtailing land ownership. Does this limitation based on the Shariah or on politics or one's own thinking? Did the problem ever come up before the old imams? Is the proposal for imposing a limit of 100 bigha in East Pakistan and of 100 to 200 acres in West Pakistan according to the Shariah?

Now when the limitation principle has been accepted as a demand of justice, will there be any hesitation from the Shariah point of view if someone imposes another limit? And the limit can also be such that feudalism is abolished altogether.

We may also consider this from another angle. There has been some hesitation in respect of unlimited land ownership and also on the permissibility of contract. If limitations on land ownership are acceptable, why should they not be so on land contract?

The right of giving land on contract, *Ikra ul ard*, is not holy; the proposal is to take this right back from the feudalist. Now all that remains to be decided is whether the absentee landlord should be allowed to exist as a relic or somehow or another get rid of his despotism and unearned income.

Along with this it may also be considered that he who has an income of Rs.1000.00 a month (assuming that the income is by permissible means), cannot purchase the shares of a large industry. What is the sanction based on the authority of former imams for placing restrictions on the permissibility of property-investment, Istighlal and Tammiyah?

Today one class is denied access to some industries and tomorrow it may be another, and so on. How can human intelligence be debarred from thinking until the shariah presents a way out? It will be dangerous to place restrictions on the investment of property, the result of which can only be wealth-concentration. One is reminded of the Quranic Verse, *Aayat ul laki*. Lurking beneath, there is an acknowledgment of the existence of class struggle.

Syed Muhammed Yusuf,

13 January 1970

Department of Arabic, Karachi University,

KARACHI.

Dr. Syed Muhammed Yusuf, (head of the Arabic Department in Karachi University) is a well-known intellectual of our country and an old patron and former Editor of al Balagh. In this article, he has raised some thoughts provoking questions and has also commented briefly on the economic programs brought forward now and again by religious organizations here. He has also permitted the Editor, al Balagh, to give his views on the relevant subjects. As these problems concern the requirements of the present day, a discussion on them is among the foremost of this journal's objectives. We shall give our own proposals too in this connection.

There are two parts to the learned Doctor's articles; one related to industry and trade and the other to agriculture.

As far as I understand him, he believes that protectionism is the main cause of the defects of capitalism. On account of the restrictions on import and export, the foreign exchange which rightfully belongs to the nation is made disposable by the industrialist who sets up his own industries with it, and when the government places restrictions on imports, by extending its 'protection' to them, his monopoly is established in the market and the masses are made to pay arbitrary prices.

Two remedies have been proposed for this state of affairs:

One, nationalization, so that the greater part of the profits the industrialist misappropriates to himself may be channelised to the people via the government and;

Two, private ownership of industry may be continued but price control should be imposed so that the industrialist may not be able to over-burden the people by fixing arbitrary prices which he does by taking advantage of his monopoly.

The learned Doctor is against the latter, both from the *Shariah* angle and on his own thinking. On the shariah basis, he builds his argument on those Traditions which oppose price control. And, logically, he believes that the consequences of price control are nothing but mischief and corruption, because of which the government plays in the hands of the capitalist or uses price control for political purposes to mislead the public.

After refuting this second proposal as well, the Doctor invites his readers to reflect whether there is any argument based in the shariah for rejecting nationalization; or is this done merely on the ulema's own logic.

In our opinion, the Doctor is right in holding that the license and permit system, restrictions on imports and industrial monopolies are a great cause of wealth concentration. In the editorial of al Balagh of Ramzan 1389 Hijra the late Maulana Mufti Muhammed Shafi wrote,

> *"The current license and permit system is a great contributory factor in the establishment of monopolies. What is happening today is that in lieu of bribes or by way of favouritism the big industrialists are given special permits, which result in establishing their self-centered monopolies in the industry and trade. This causes the prices to rise and prevents people with small capital to enter the market". (P. 6)*

In our opinion, neither nationalization nor price control can remedy this state of affairs. An Islamic government should break up monopolies and replace them with free competition so that the prices of goods and services may find their own level on the basis of their utility and intrinsic value. To achieve this end, the following steps need to be taken:

1. Trade should gradually be made free, and restrictions on imports and exports lifted;
2. Interest, gambling and speculation should be totally banned;
3. The economy should be run on principles of co-sharing and mudar-e-but, so that the benefit of money deposited in the banks may accrue to the people and not just a few capitalists or industrialists.
4. Cartels and such agreements should be eliminated.

Price Control:

The proposals being made by the ulema for price control as opposed to nationalization, are not according to the real purpose of Islam. They are meant only for a transitory period to meet the emergency of the moment. It is not denied that Islam requires that prices take their own natural course according to the laws of supply and demand. This is confirmed by a Tradition reported by Abu Huraira and another by Anas quoted by the Doctor. Imam Abu Hanifa does not hold price control to be permissible. The difficulty today is that breaking up monopolies and replacing them with free competition could not be done overnight.

Undoubtedly the present restrictions on imports and exports are contributing to the unbalanced distribution of wealth, but if foreign trade were totally freed where would the required foreign exchange come from? Therefore, before making foreign trade unrestricted the difficulties of acquiring free trade would have to be resolved and this will take time. One cannot wait for the daily bread indefinitely and, therefore, to help the masses against high prices, something will have to be done for the intervening period. Price control will have to be tolerated as a transitory measure; that is, until the monopolies are completely extinct. For this reason alone, the Islamic jurists, fuqaha, permit price control. Imam Abu Hanifa is well known as an opponent of price control, yet he states:

فإن كان أربابُ الطعامِ يتحكَّمون، ويتعدَّون عن القيمةِ تعدِّيًا فاحشا، وعجزَ القاضي عن صيانةِ حقوقِ المسلمين إلا بالتسعير، فحينئذٍ لا بأسَ به، بمشورةِ أهلِ الرأيِ والبصيرة.

"If the owners of food-grain become monopolists and go beyond the limits and the qadi finds himself unable to secure the rights of the Muslims without imposing practice control, he may do so after consulting the men of vision and the opinion- worthy."

These words show that price control is justified only as a compulsion of the circumstances. But when monopolies cease to exist and the national economy reverts to its natural free processes, price control becomes repugnant. Therefore, it is the duty of an Islamic government to endeavour to establish free trade and conditions of free enterprise so that prices may adjust themselves by the natural processes and their control may not be required.

Islam and Restrictions on Imports and Exports:

The learned Doctor asks, "From the shariah point of view, how is the government justified in compelling the common consumer to purchase goods manufactured by one or more industrialists at prices fixed arbitrarily by them? Can a single instance be found of such action during the time of the Prophet or of the first four Caliphs, the *Rashideen*?

As we have said, this method does not accord with Islamic principles, and the Prophet preferred leaving foreign trade free and unhampered. Imam Dar Qutni, Baihaqi, Abul Ya'la and Tabrani quote from the Lady Ayesha (Radhi Allahu Anha) and Abdullah from Ibn Abu Ayash b. Rabi' a:

اطلبو الرزق في خيابا الارض

"Search a livelihood in all the corners of the earth."

Tabrani also quotes from Sharjeel b. al- Samat:

من تعذرت عليه التجارة فعليه بعمان

"He whose trade becomes difficult should go away to Amman."

And yet another Tradition advises migration to Egypt.

(Kanz ul Amaal N. 4174).

The trade journey can be for both import and export purposes. No restrictions on free foreign trade is found during the Prophet's time or that of His immediate Caliphs; rather, encouragement to it is not wanting. From the purely juristic angle, it is an act of great cruelty that the wealth earned by the people with their blood and sweat should be transferred to the big capitalists while they, the people, are given more paper currency notes. This is a kind of hajar and permissibility of which is beyond our understanding.

No reputable scholar, as far as I know, has sanctioned such persecution, though he has been troubled by the thought of the difficulty of acquiring foreign exchange, if foreign trade were made totally free.

This should be the economist's headache. Protection is being opposed not only by the ulema but by the economists as well. Probably, there is no region of this globe where this opposition is not being aired. If an Islamic government is ever established, it will resolve the difficulty with the help of the economists. It may review the entire gambit of the monetary system to restore it on the lines of the gold standard.

Nationalization:

The problems created by capitalism can be resolved only by the means we have just stated, namely, banning interest, gambling, speculation, etc., and creating an atmosphere of free competition to enable wealth to circulate over an ever-increasing wider circle. Nationalization, which is a recommendation of Western philosophers, is no more than a hotchpotch complication. It is true that the objections which the ulema have made so far are based on their own intellectual logic and are not based in the shariah; but this is not because there is no Shariah objections to it but because the reputation of it from the Shariah angle is so self-evident that they do not consider it necessary to debate about it. We should like to make it clear that we are talking about nationalization of property earned in legitimate ways. For the government to take possession of such property is gross injustice and tyranny. Consider the Verse.

﴿لَا تَأْكُلُوٓاْ أَمْوَٰلَكُم بَيْنَكُم بِٱلْبَٰطِلِ إِلَّآ أَن تَكُونَ تِجَٰرَةً عَن تَرَاضٍ مِّنكُمْۚ﴾ [النساء: 29]

"Do not devour one another's wealth by false means but (acquire it) by mutual agreement such as by trade."

The following words from the address on the occasion of the Last Pilgrimage also support this view:

ألا إن دمائكم وأموالكم وأعراضكم حرام عليكم كحرمة يومكم هذا، في بلدكم هذا، في شهركم هذا.

But your blood, your wealth, and your honour are as sacred to you as this day of yours in this country of yours, in this month.

This is the same احزاموال الناس قهراً which the Doctor himself holds to be impermissible. Therefore, it is obvious that nationalization is impermissible. Since the time of the Prophet until the present day there has not been a jurist, faqih, worth mentioning who has held nationalization to be permissible. If there is anyone who does so, let him come forward with a shariah-based proof.

The fact is that nationalization is based on Karl Mark's ideas of 'surplus value' according to which all income, except labor wage, is impermissible, whether interest, profit or rent. If this idea is accepted, nationalization, no doubt is sensible because the capitalist's income with which he builds his industry comes, for the greater part, from interest, profit and rent, and since all these media from the surplus value angle are illegitimate, his whole industry is rendered illegitimate, Therefore, to seize the industry and vest it in public ownership is but a logical consequence of the process. But, if the idea of surplus value is held to be invalid, that part of the capitalist's income which he earns as profit and rent is legitimate. To seize the whole, then, is not valid by any logic whatsoever.

The problem is not that of national ownership but of surplus value. What we have to see basically is whether surplus value is according to Islam or not. If it is according to Islam, its permissibility will have to be admitted, but if it is not, nationalization is meaningless.

And now, looking at surplus value we find that it is wrong in its very concept, because it holds that all income from profit and rent included, but not from labor wage is illegitimate, whereas, Islam holds labor wage, profit and rent to be equally legitimate. Of the four media of income, it holds only interest to be illegitimate.

Not in one but several places have the Quran declared profit from trade to be blessing of Allah. All the offshoots of buying and selling, contract, co-sharing, *Mudarbah* and many other relevant principles are derived from the permissibility of profit and rent. This is so clear that, in many opinions, there is no point in advancing detailed arguments about it.

When it is proved that the concept of surplus value is opposed to Islam and only that income of industrialist is invalid which is derived from interest, speculation and gambling or any other such means, it is, without doubt, permissible to such property. But, if the income be from profit and rent, such property is without doubt legitimate, and, after holding it as legitimate, it may not be seized in whole, but the government may take from it only such dues as *zaka't* and *Ushr*, etc.

Today, those people who are great champions of nationalization should present us their views on surplus value. Thinking of nationalization, a suspicion of atheism comes to the mind because the thought of nationalization is derived from the concept of surplus value, and the concept of surplus value is opposed to the basics of the Shariah and is not admissible as a subject of (Islamic) juristic.

We are well aware that propaganda media have made nationalization indispensable to development, and there are among us those elements who are trying to prove that Riba (usury, interest etc.,) and socialism, both are in consonance with Islam, but the ulema are prepared to put up with being mocked as 'reactionary' and 'obsolete' rather than yield even the slightest in matters of the absolute basics of Islam.

As for the ulema themselves advancing that some industries should be run by the government, the reference, probably, is to Maulana Mufti Muhammed Shafi's words published in al Balagh. Ramzan '89 AH:

> *"Key industries, such as the railways, shipping, shipbuilding, steel, oil and such, should be established by the government under its own supervision and the shares sold only to those whose income in less than Rs. 1000.00 per month."*

A misunderstanding seems to have been created because of some words here. Some people, besides the Doctor, have drawn our attention to this. We shall explain what the Mufti Sahab really intended. All that has been said is that the key industries existing at present were established by the government and are semi- government owned, but practically all the shares of the public sector are owned by the big capitalists and the profits of the industries nationalized from the beginning go to them. If the government were to alter this state of affairs and announce that the shares of such industries will be given only to those people, whose incomes are less than Rs. 1000.00 a month, the general public, instead of the capitalist, would benefit from their profits.

Doing this is permissible according to the shariah because these industries, from the beginning, are government-established. Therefore, the government has a right to make agreements with or refuse whomsoever it pleases; just as any individual has the right to do. This proposition is entirely different from nationalization, because nationalization means that an industry is established by someone else, and then the government seizes it to itself by force.

This explanation should dispel the Doctor's other dilemma about the imposition of restriction on the investment of wealth with reference to the authority of the old imams. The intention is not to impose restrictions on investment but to clarify that every businessman has the right to select whomsoever he wants for his partnership. Today governments lay down conditions about those it will sell the shares to. This is not the same as imposing restrictions on investment.

Contract Lands:

In the second part of his article, the Doctor proposes that to put end to injustices, the contract system should be abolished, and such limits should be imposed on ownership of rural land and feudalism that it may ultimately cease to exist.

It is admitted that Ibn Hazam has held the system of giving land on contract in return for money as impermissible, but, in view of the many Traditions to the contrary, it is difficult to agree with him. Not only are Imam Abu Hanifa, Shafa'1, Malik and Ahmed opposed to his views but almost every other jurist and alim too. There is not a single Companion of the Holy Prophet who agrees to it. Shaukani, who supports Ibn Hazam on many issues, disagrees with him on this. He writes on Ibn Manzar's authority:

إن الصحابة أجمعوا على جوز كراء الأرض بالذهب والفضة ونقل ابن بطال اتفاق فقهاء الأمصار عليه

The Companions unanimously agreed on the permissibility of renting land for gold and silver, and Ibn Battal quoted the agreement of the Egyptian jurists on this.

"All the Companions are unanimously agreed that land may be rented out for gold and silver returns, and Ibn Abtal has recorded the agreement in every region, including the practice of those Companions on whose reported Tradition Ibn Hazam bases his argument. The world of learning knows that Ibn Hazam has not been accepted on many subjects."

The Doctor quotes Ibn Hazam's opinion for putting an end to the feudalist's tyranny. But if this opinion were accepted, giving land on rent for cultivation would be legitimate but contract would be illegitimate, though in our society, the peasants are victims of feudalist tyranny. There are very few cases of peasants taking land on contract for cultivation. Besides, contractors are not so bound up to the feudalist's power as the peasants are, whom centuries of tradition have reduced to the position of serfs.

The Doctor's proposal, even if accepted, could not be of much avail for the general good. In our view, the only cure for the feudalist's tyranny is that published in the editorial of al Balagh, Ramzan 89 AH.

Curtailing Ownership of Land:

Finally, the Doctor has raised the question of curtailing the ownership of land. This implies limiting the size of the holdings per individual to a certain number of square yards or acres and taking the surplus away from the holders. Today, this is what is commonly taken as reducing the ownership of land. Even the opponents of socialism advance this method as a solution.

But, in our opinion, this is neither in accordance with the Shariah nor can it be of any help in the present conditions to achieve the purpose of limitation. During the time of the former President Muhammed Ayub Khan a limit of 500 acres had been imposed, but today thousands and thousands of acres are still vested in one individual. The big feudalists have transferred parts of their land to the peasants who do not even know that their names are entered in the official documents.

There are other ways of curtailing ownership by which no limit is placed in terms of measurement, but, if acted upon, big areas of feudalist land are automatically reduced to reasonable limits and the harm being done to the poor because of feudalism will also be taken care of. Islam lays stress on such methods for keeping wealth, whether in the shape of money or property, within proper limits and places no specific bounds anywhere. The limit of 100 or 200 acres proposed by certain parties are against the Shariah, no example of it being found in the fourteen centuries of the ummah's history. However, in the present social conditions, the following methods may well be adopted to divide large areas of land:

a) Implementing the Islamic law of inheritance in respect of those lands in which the owners have so far evaded it, so that appropriate parts of the land may be transferred to the rightful owners.

b) Strictly enforcing the Islamic law of inheritance in future.

c) Land which can be proved to have been acquired by illegitimate means should be seized and distributed among the poor. Land mortgaged on illegitimate terms (today practically all such lands are held on illegitimate terms) should be released and returned to the borrower.

d) Transfer of land from hand to hand should be facilitated, and its free sale and purchase encouraged.

Such steps alone can reduce big land holdings to smaller, reasonable units. It should also be remembered that the law alone does not accomplish everything. It is very difficult to reform conditions after creating class struggle and enmity among the parties. If hatred is cooled down, the bonhomie and goodwill, side by side of the law, can do much to resolve problems by mutual agreement. If the nation that declared its hidden wealth in 1958 is taken into confidence and its mind trained properly, there is no reason why it should not of its own accord gladly present all the land above its requirements to be taken away. Besides, landowners can also be persuaded to give parts of their land on compensation.

A similar situation had arisen during the time of the second Caliph Omer, when, instead of seizing the lands, the entire Bajola clan was persuaded on the basis of brotherhood, to dispose of them, some without and some with compensation. This method can be followed today also.

We have presented our views here with brevity. Al Balagh welcomes anyone who may wish to express his views in its pages on the subject.

اللهم أرنا الحق حقا وارزقنا اتباعه وأرنا الباطل باطلا وارزقنا اجتنابه

Socialism and the Poor

The Salient Points of the Islamic socio-economic order have been dealt with in the last chapter. A careful study of them will oblige the reader to conclude that if this order is implemented, the cruel vagaries of the distribution of wealth would cease to exist. In any case, a compelling answer is elicited to the question regarding the order that Islam proposes for satisfying the economic needs of the poor and how conditions for general social welfare can be created.

In all fairness, we should now like to ask the champions of socialism, what good does their theory do for the common poverty poverty-stricken man? How will it benefit the average individual? If implemented, how will the social wealth reach the hands of the poor? And what measures can it take to prevent concentration of wealth in a few hands?

The socialists have no reasonable answers to these questions. The fact is that socialism is a negative movement and to this day has never been able to present a sufficiently thought-out blueprint. It has raised slogans of economic equality, made great claims of sympathy for the poor, achieved considerable success in creating hatred against the tyranny of the feudo-capitalist system, but it has never come forward with any positive programme to show what it proposes to do about this tyranny and persecution; what will be the practical means to relieve the poor from the yoke of capitalism; or how economic equality will be established under a socialist regime.

Some readers may be astonished at these words because socialism has introduced itself to the world. as an economic movement and the rest has been left for propaganda to achieve the impression that socialism is the only cure for the injustices of capitalism, and if it is implemented, all the evils of capitalism will ipso facto come to an end.

Those readers who have studied socialist literature know that all this is nothing but propaganda. Socialism has rendered no service against capitalism except verbal hatred. Socialist literature is full of such words as the following:

"The Capitalists are sucking the blood of the workers". "All the nation's wealth has concentrated in the hands of the few.": "capitalist plunder cannot be tolerated at any price.... "Factories should belong to labor and land to the peasants......."; "labor creates wealth but the capitalist appropriates it to himself...."; "in a people's government, there is no room for millionaires."; "we will not rest until we get labor its due right.". and so on and so forth.

But what practical relief and recourse socialism has for dealing with the masses is not known. How will the imbalance of wealth-distribution be put right? After nationalizing the means of production how will labor and peasant be relieved of their difficulties? How practically will their government be established? How will economic equality be achieved?

These are questions that have been submerged in the noise of political slogans, and if someone tries to resolve them intelligently, the socialists react by accusing him of being "an American agent".

Socialism is based on Karl Mark's Das Kapital, known as the Bible of Communism. This book comprising three volumes should be read through and through. It is full of philosophical criticism of capitalism and, except some vague hints and suggestions, has nothing in it.

If socialism has any positive strategy worth the name to offer, it is this: nationalize all means of production and establish a planned economy in which the use of the means of production and the distribution of wealth will be according to the government's planning. It is this proposal that is being propagated with great fanfare as if nationalization were some magic lamps that would dispel all darknesses of tyranny and persecution as soon as it was lighted up. The factory laborer and the peasant are made to understand that nationalization means their ownership of the factory and land and there will be no upper hand of the capitalist over them. It is, indeed, a miracle of communist propaganda that this white lie is believed by all and sundry. Even sworn opponents of socialism sometimes fall under its spell and begin to demand nationalization. Few stops to think how possibly can labor become owner of a factory or the peasant owner of land.

All that nationalization does is transfer the individually owned factory and land to the government. What beneficial change does this change of masters bring to labour and peasant? Formerly, the individual owner paid wages in return for services, and now, it is the government that pays wages for the same services. Labor had no right of interference in the factory management, and he has none under the government, he had no ownership rights in the profits before and has none later; salaries were not fixed on labor's free will before and are not fixed according to their free will now. Where then is the paradise which was not his in the slavery to the former employer, but he now occupies under slavery to the government?

It is said that after bringing the factories under his control, the government of the day will be his government, and as such, will deal with him with justice, and will not be able to deprive him of his rights. So now let us see what the government of the working classes means under socialism.

Communist propaganda has tried to make the simple-minded people believe that "the workers government" implies that the tiller of the soil and machine-man of a lathe will immediately occupy government chairs and being in absolute power, will be able to turn every hut and hearth in the country into a marble palace. But let us see what this government's face is like.

Of the millions of laborers and peasants in the country, there will be a party comprising only a few individuals, not more than three or four per cent of them.

This party will select a few from within itself to make a ministry which will be the real absolute master of the country. The ministers will control all the factories and land; formulate every policy, fix salaries and wages and prices of all goods; while the party that appointed the ministers will be able to do no more than meet once or twice a year, ratify the government's policies and, at the most, offer some criticism. As for the millions who deceived themselves by hopes of forming their government and surrendered their all to the party will find themselves deprived of any right to question the government's policies or dare speak a word against its decisions.

If those in power so decide, the party will not meet for years, as happens in the Soviets.

If a handful of the country's rulers who control every factory, every inch of land, all the means of production and other treasures, buy up the party members, not a soul is left with courage enough to speak a word in opposition.

We saw a glimpse of this in the Basic Democracies of the last regime, how millions of the electorate become helpless after transferring their power to a few thousand BD members. These members and their elected assembles could do no more than underspin whatever the government wished. The difference was that though the rights of the electorate for the greater part were confiscated, the right to demonstrations strikes, holding meetings, and taking out processions remained intact and on that account, after ten years, the people succeeded in changing the government. But under socialism, they will have no right to form a party or to go on strike, hold meetings or demonstrations or take out processions --- such things are not part of socialism --; a bird caged and shorn of its wings so that it may not even flutter freely.

Such is the workers' government for which labor and peasant are being advised to sacrifice their lives and property. Anyone who obstructs the establishment of such a government is an agent of imperialism and enemy of the workers who should be eliminated at all costs.

Now consider what labor's condition will be in such. conditions. Let us assume that a worker finds his wages insufficient or not commensurate with his labor. What ways and means has he open before him under socialism's so-called workers' government? He cannot form a trade union; he cannot go on strike; demonstrations are forbidden for him. All this because demonstrations, strikes, trade unions are relics of capitalism; now when the workers' own government has been established, how can they be permitted to resort to those means!

The worker may now think of going to a director and applying to him for an increase of his wages. But the director is not the owner of a factory to increase or decrease any workers wages. His curt answer is that increasing wages is not in his power, only the government can do that. The worker now goes to knock at the government's door, but it is extremely difficult to draw the attention of a government busy with such important tasks as protecting the "larger interests of labor" and exercising day and night for "a world government of all workers" and it has no time to listen to such petty matters as wage increase. But let us suppose the dissatisfied man does succeed in contacting the proper minister or official, the response he gets there is that the means required for establishing a workers' world government are not yet available and will not be available until the workers sacrifice their personal interests. Therefore, the exigency of the interests of the workers requires that wages may not be increased and, denying themselves even a good part of the daily bread, they should strive to liberate and bring those workers under the protection of the "workers' government" who are still being trodden down under capitalism!

So, this last hope too is shattered to pieces. Should he now think that the "workers' government" is making a fool of him and there is no way out for him, there is no political party which he may approach for redress. He cannot, either leave his present job and take another because every other factory too belongs to the "workers' government". He cannot say farewell to his profession, because the "workers' government" has selected his profession for him after due consideration and he cannot leave this profession without permission from above. Now the wretch has no alternative but to strive all his life patiently for a wage fixed for him by "his own" government and never again think of a wage increase because he may be sent to prison on suspicion of being an enemy of labor's interests or a capitalist spy.

Such are the consequences of nationalization and a socialist government to a worker. Should the facts detailed here appear incorrect to anyone, let him come forward to tell us what the alternatives open to a worker are for wage increase, change of profession or securing his other rights. What guarantee is there for getting a fair share in he factory profits? How may a government be changed when by dishonesty or mistake it adopts oppressive policies? What restrictions are imposed on the unlimited powers of the government? By whom and according to what standard are the wages fixed? To what extent are the opinions of labor effective in such determination? Until satisfactory answers to these questions are presented the mere name "workers' government" cannot fill the worker's hungry stomach.

As against this, reforms under an Islamic social order directly make the workers owners of the factory and, as co-sharers, recipients of proportionate profits. More ways of earning an income and less of spending are open to the people. If the socialists are sincerely interested in the workers and the poor, why do they not accept this way for the welfare of the workers, a way beneficial for them and also according to Islam?

Islam, Democracy, and Socialism

"Islam is our religion;

Democracy is our policy;

Socialism is our economy."

This is the slogan, which some political parties are broadcasting with great fanfare in the country. The first word 'Islam' in this slogan is meant to give the impression that Islam is accorded priority in the new social order. But this is wholly deceptive. It is like placing someone on a throne after amputating his arms and legs!

The first thought that comes to one's mind on reading these lines is that Islam, like Christianity or Hinduism, is the name of a few random principles and rituals of worship, and has nothing to do with the political, economic, social or other problems of life. It is enough to adopt these principles and rituals and then, one is free to live by whichever economy or form of government he pleases. Sitting in a mosque, he is bound by religious precepts but outside, in matters administrative or seeking a livelihood, Islam has given either no directives or such defective ones that we are obliged to look elsewhere for the right guidance: democracy in matters political, socialism in matters economic.

That being so, why do they say alongside the Islam is a complete 'code of life' and it contains the solution to every human problem?

They should come out openly to declare that Islam has given them no guidance except in matters of worship and some beliefs, and though they hold the Quran within their hearts, they are compelled to turn to Marx and Mao Se Tung for guidance.

And if they claim that the teachings of Islam are not confined to worship and beliefs but include all that is required in life, they will have to follow Islam everywhere, mosque, or market, government office or place of entertainment. It makes no sense that in the mosque they should turn their faces towards the Ku'ba, but in the market or office make Moscow and Peking their focal centre. They will have to look at the countenance of that great benefactor of humanity whose teachings lighted up not only mosques but also government palaces and markets.

Some people interpret this slogan to assert that the socialism implied here is not irreligious socialism but Islamic socialism. Just as democracy can be Islamic, so can socialism be Islamic.

Our contention is that as technical names both Islamic democracy and Islamic socialism are wrong. Both are concepts of western irreligious thinking. To patch on Islam on them is an affront to Islam. It also creates the impression that both are identical with Islam, which they are not.

But in their literal meaning, there is a difference of earth and sky between the two. In the philosophic concept of democracy there are some thoughts that are against Islam, for instance, the supremacy of the people, the ultimate authority of the legislature without any binding qualification of Divine commands, or a candidate's demanding power and government. But there are several principles of democracy which accord with Islam and the people recognize as basic, for instance, government by consultation, division of offices, free expression of opinion, government's responsibility to the people, and such. Those people who use the term 'Islamic democracy' understand that only such democratic nations are intended as do not conflict with Islam.

As against this, the champions of 'Islamic socialism' assert that there is nothing intrinsically wrong with the term, except that its first projectors were atheists and they appended Islam to their socialism. Now, if Islam is added to socialism, that is, if the economics of socialism are adopted and belief in God and the Prophet and faith in the hereafter are added, socialism becomes Islamic.

And they claim that they have purged out all un-Islamic elements from socialism and have named it as "Islamic Socialism". This assertion is wrong because in their socialism every feature of the economic order is retained that in altogether un-Islamic. Socialism is based on seizure by force of all the means of production, and this concept is included in Islamic Socialism, as proclaimed repeatedly in speeches and writings. Besides, socialism is not only a philosophy but also an economic system which, beginning to end, is wholly un-Islamic. Therefore, if the un-Islamic parts are deducted from socialism, nothing is left in the balance to give it a name.

Let us take an example. The term 'Islamic democracy' is like 'Islamic banking. Banking today is conducted on the basis of surcharging interest on loans, which is thoroughly un-Islamic. But, if banking is done without interest and on the lines of *Mudarbah*, it accords with the principles of the Islamic social order. The name may still be objected to but in the literal meaning of the words it is not objectionable.

'Islamic Socialism', however, is different; like 'Islamic usury' or 'Islamic gambling', both ridiculous terms, because usury or interest and gambling are intrinsically and wholly un-Islamic. They cannot be modified so as to be purged of their impure element, minus which nothing is left to patch the un-Islamic label on to them.

It is also argued that the term 'Islamic Socialism' is used only to make it clear that Islam is not capitalism. Some people try to prove that it is. This logic is weak. It is not being intelligent to replace one misunderstanding with another. If the motive is really to emphasize that

Islam does not support exploitation and persecution, some other terms should be employed, Islamic Social Justice, or such.

In the slogan, socialism and democracy have quite innocently been compounded with one another, as if there was no conflict between the two, although the fact is that the road taken by *Ishtirakiat*, communism is nowhere near democracy. Islam, indeed, does oppose that wealth should be concentrated in a few hands, and it does stand for its circulation over the widest field, but to do this it does not tolerate the tyrannical way taken by socialism. The result of seizing the means of production from the people and consigning them to a few individuals of the government can only be to place all the nation's wealth in the hands of a huge capitalist party while the masses are rendered more impoverished than ever before. Therefore, Islam cannot go along with a socialism that is based on denial of the principle of private ownership.

Similarly, the history of socialism shows that democracy has never gone along with it. The spirit of democracy is free expression of opinion, while socialism is merely a slogan that has no existence in a world of facts. It has always been implemented by force after brutal suppression of free expression; it has never tolerated criticism because its planned economy is not possible without a ruthless dictatorship; Consider that in a socialist country no political party other than the Communist is permitted to exist; labor cannot form its own organization to vindicate its rights, and there is no freedom of the press. How then can the word 'democracy' be used for a socialist society?

We are well aware that many genuine Muslims have fallen in line with the socialist slogan but that is only because the word 'Islamic' is attached to it. We draw their attention to the history of Islamic Socialism to consider the atrocities it has inflicted on Islam and the Muslims and how the Islamic values have been trampled on. There is no denying that the evils of capitalism are repugnant and every throbbing heart should cherish the zeal to destroy them, but it should be remembered that the laborer and peasant will find peace and satisfaction only in the lap of that personality, who never ate food to the fill of his appetite and was ever anxious for the welfare of the poor.

It is not wisdom to come out of the frying pan and deliberately fall into the fire!

Socialism and Economic Equality

The reader may have observed that economic equality has no factual existence in the socialism. There is a gap of 110 and 30,000 in the pay scales. In other words, the salaries of the top officers are 300 times that of the average laborer. If this is economic equality, God alone knows that class differences should mean. It is obvious that 'economic equality' is only a slogan, and the worst of class differences exist also in the communist countries.

Islam, on the other hand, has never made false claims for economic equality. Islam is a religion of natural facts, *deen e fitrat*. It is not blind to the fact that equality of incomes for all human beings is impossible, just as there are natural differences of intelligence, beauty, health, energy and strength between man and man. As long as there are differences of natural talent, there will be differences of individual income. No social structure can demolish these differences. Man's vision may be deceived sometimes, but this law of nature is unchangeable. It may appear at times that a laborer who shovels mud gets so little for his labor, while the engineer earns many times more. A superficial man may think that this is not justice. But seeing things deeper, it will have to be concluded that what the engineer earns are not for a day's labor but that of years and years of blood and sweat for qualifying for his degrees.

Islam has never denied the natural differences to announce economic equality, but it has prescribed ways and means to curb the natural tendencies from going too far and assuming the tyrannical proportions of capitalism.

To do this, Islam proposes that the prices of consumer goods and services should fix themselves in the free competition market. The fact is that there is no better way of keeping natural differences within reasonable and just limits, there being no man-made criterion measure for achieving this. Therefore, just as the differences of utility and intrinsic value are natural, and there is no measure to judge them by, so also is it above human beings to fix the differences of market prices. Only the natural laws of supply and demand can determine the differences.

This is the natural process which being obstructed brings about great differences of income between man and man. In the capitalist system, interest, speculation and gambling put an end to free competition to establish monopolies and the laws of supply and demand become paralyzed, unable to be of any avail to the common man, the prices not finding their own fixture but forced to the capitalist's planning for his own benefit. The inevitable result is an excessive widening of the income gap, pumping the wealth to the capitalists and drying up the channels leading to the commoners.

The correct way to deal with this was for the socialists to put an end to the monopolies and their causes, namely, interest, speculation, permit system, and establish free competition to allow the laws of supply and demand to take their free course and fixed prices accordingly. But what socialism did was to replace all this with its own artificial, arbitrary structure in which the government subordinated the laws of supply and demand to artificial planning and fixed prices and wages as it willed.

In the beginning this procedure was adopted because it was planned to eliminate every vestige of differences of income, and announcements were made accordingly, but when it was found that the natural process of inequality incomes could not be controlled, it was decided to have recourse to "reasonable differences", Marx being opposed to equality socialism, as it was said. But there was no barometer to ascertain what was reasonable and what was not --- the interplay of supply and demand had already been banned --- and the planned economy system which was presumed to the elastic enough to correspond with the personal wishes or views of the bureaucrats could not replace the natural laws. So, when the door opened on the differences, the gap went on widening more and more. The argument that justified a ratio of five to ten was increased to five to fifteen, and the process went on until the difference were as great as obtained in the capitalist countries.

What is now clear is that both capitalism and communism rebel against the natural process of economics and each tries to build its own artificial structure. Therefore, balance and moderation could not be achieved by either. However, sincerely socialism might try to eliminate the differences between poverty and riches, by ignoring the natural laws, it had to revert to the position it tried to escape.

Because Islam has kept the demand and supply order free of artificial limits, it never made any false claims to economic equality but controls inequalities within such channels that the national wealth automatically circulates by a well-balanced process and that tremendous rich-poor gap which exists in capitalist societies and inevitably also comes about in the socialist, does not materialize here.

We have just stated that Islam has never advocated economic equality. The equality which Muslims have always very proudly proclaimed is social equality, not economic equality. No one is superior or inferior on the basis of his birth or status or wealth. Everyone is equal before the law and has equal opportunities to earn his daily bread. None holding monopolies of wealth has the right to block another's path of making a living; but one is no criminal if, because of his superior intelligence, he earns more than another does by honest means. His income is permissible and clean, and Islam protects it in every way. Differences of income arising in this way are within Islam. Such differences existed during the time of the Prophet and of his companions and throughout the history of Islam. The income differences, however, made no differences to the civic and social rights of the rich and poor. The rights that belonged to the companions like Usman Ghani, Abdul Rehman b. Auf or Zubair bin Awwam also belonged to Abu Huraira, Salman Farsi and Bilal Habshi. Indeed, there were some among the slaves and the poor who, because of their piety and superior intelligence, were appointed to the highest offices of the state.

This also shows that those people who refer to Islamic equality in support of socialism are far from being right. Islam has never laid any claims to establish the economic equality which socialism holds as its ideal (but which it has never achieved so far nor even can). Islam's equality is social equality which cannot be advanced to support socialism.

Socialist Objections

We have expressed our opinion about socialism, not once, but many times. No social order and no concept or slogan other than Islam will ever be acceptable to the people of Pakistan. The capitalist order of Europe and United States of America, or the socialist order of Russia and Chine can find no favour here. The majority of the people here would like to see Islam implemented which the Prophet brought to the world. Therefore, if slogans are constantly sung in support of communism or socialism it is every citizen's natural right to air his opposition and condemn every movement that seeks to implement any non-Islamic theory.

Writing against communism was our natural right. There were counter-objections, some of them the stereotyped ones which the socialists and communists use over the world against their opponents, and some intellectual, not propaganda stuff. We appreciate these and answer them in our pages here, inviting others also to send us their views freely expressed on this subject. In-sha Allah, we shall answer them with absolute sincerity.

As for the former, the slogans have been coined solely for propaganda purposes, not for intellectual investigation or debate. It is, therefore, useless to deal with them. They are meant only to create hatred, and nothing said or written against them will ever put a stop to their wild singing. However, since some simple-minded people may fall for them, we may briefly acquaint them with the reality.

The first criticism raised in the stereotyped phraseology is that we are "capitalist agents" and are championing the cause of capitalism in opposition to the labor movement.

As said before, we are not only target of this censure. It has to be heard by everyone who has anything to say against communism. Communists keep accusing the ulema of supporting the capitalists against the working classes.

But this is a white lie which none with the least sense in him will be foolish enough to believe. If by capitalism is meant that order which has been forced on us by the West and which has sucked every drop of the poor man's blood to foster a few individuals, let them give us the name of one alim who ever supported such a tyrannical economy. In the past two-hundred years of India's history the first voice to rise against imperialism was that of the ulema who sacrificed their lives and possessions to thwart the political and intellectual domination of India by the West. Who is there that can claim to have made greater sacrifices in this matter?

Instead of cursing capitalism and merely sounding some objections, what the ulema did was to go to the very root of the evils of capitalism. They found that interest, speculation, gambling and hoarding were the causes of these evils which pumped all the wealth to the capitalists while the poor starved. Therefore, since the establishment of Pakistan, the ulema devoted themselves with one accord to rid the country of these evils and replace them with the balanced economy of Islam. For their efforts, they were accused of being "reactionaries", "obsolete", "narrow-minded", but no word of abuse could stop them from speaking out what they considered to be the truth. Those people who today are professing their hatred of capitalism and claim to be sympathetic for the poor are the ones who in those days felt no pain in their heats for the poverty stricken and who supported the capitalist socio-economics, obstructing the ulema in the performance of their work.

It is strange logic that those elements who helped maintain the basic causes of the evils of capitalism were not styled as "agents of capitalism", but those who did their best to eliminate interest, speculation, hoarding and gambling were called its supporters and "agents"! Those who were advocates of usurious loans and mortgages were not taken for guardians of feudalism; those who left the national economy to the mercy of the speculators were not looked upon as guilty of the crime of allying with the capitalist order; those who obstructed the path of the greatest opponents of capitalism were not accused of supporting capitalism; --- but those ulema who from the first day fought valiantly every evil of capitalism and did their best to uproot capitalism and establish Islam's just social order were accused of being "agents of capitalism".---- only because they did not approve the communist oppression as a substitute for the injustices of capitalism!

The truth is that no one has done more to oppose capitalism than the ulema. The writings and speeches of the ulema are there to prove that they have constantly endeavoured to eradicate the despotic social order. They are its opponents today and shall always remain its opponents. But they believe that the only way to accomplish this is to implement the Islamic life order in its totality because the solution that Islam possesses to resolve the evils of capitalism is not to be found in any other social system.

Specially the road taken by Socialism to fight capitalism is extremely harmful, dangerous and destructive. Like capitalism, socialism too is a creature of Western materialism. It places the destiny of the masses in the hands of a few government officials who control not only their monetary wealth but also their hearts, minds and consciences, their emotions and desires, who use them as machine tools, and after depriving them of their very hearts and souls, take away even their tongues with which they might complain!

The thoroughly inhuman social order is in reality a form, the worst form of capitalism, in which one big capitalist devouring several small capitalists, becomes more ruinous for the masses. That is why we consider it necessary to fight capitalism and socialism together, otherwise the result will be only to force a bigger evil on the people after relieving them of a smaller.

Now if anyone, who looks up this as supporting capitalism and gives us all manner of nicknames, he is welcome to do so. Nothing can deter us from proclaiming the truth. We are seeing with our own eyes the abysses into with our people are fraudulently being pushed. We are well aware of the shackles that are being prepared to chain them to communist dictatorship. Therefore, we shall go on proclaiming that the road to liberation from capitalism is not by socialism but through Islam.

One very peculiar objection being levelled, is that denouncing socialism will adversely affect our relations with the communist countries. China helped us during the September 1965 war with India, therefore, we should say nothing about its socio-economics.

Such criticism can come only from one who can distinguish between political friendship and intellectual slavery. It is good to maintain cordial relations with the communist countries, but how does this mean that we should subordinate our religion, culture, heart and soul to communism? And should any one cry slogans such as "Down with Islam" we should not venture to silence his voice?

Every country maintains diplomatic, trade, military and political relations with another country, and at the same time there is criticism of principles and views on the intellectual level. We have never heard that wherever such relations exist, there should also be not only acceptance of the other's theories, but also their import to make them part of the constitution and laws of one's own country, and if someone should want to do so nothing should be said against it.

If attempts were made to enforce Islam in China or Russia would, they remain silent because of mutual good relations with Pakistan or other

Muslim country? Is not Islam already criticized and censured there? Have they expressed their acceptance of Islam on the basis of friendly relations? If the answer is in the negative, why should our conscience be so dead that we surrender even our right to defend our beliefs?

If someone advises us to adopt communist views because of our friendly relations with the communist countries, although they may not convert to our views, what can the reason be but that the communist countries are stronger than us. Probably, this is what communism teaches; that every weakling should submit not only its outward form but also its beliefs, thoughts, heart, and conscience to the strong!

Agricultural Reforms

Today the agricultural reforms of the present government are being talked about as its pride achievement, a maximum limit of 150 acres being fixed for land ownership, but the question is whether this will put an end to the injustices prevailing in this sector. How can it be presumed that the person who possesses 150 acres must have come by it in the permissible process or that he will not oppress his peasants? And he who owns an acre more than 150 acres must have come by it in impermissible ways, and he must be tyrannizing over his peasants; and if he surrenders the surplus one acre, his tyranny too must simultaneously come to an end.

As we see the problem, the real issue is the oppression of the peasant at the hands of the feudalist who has turned him into a virtual slave. To put an end to the oppression what should have been done in the Islamic way was, instead of limiting ownership, to distribute those lands among the rightful owners which a feudalist has come to possess by impermissible means, about which the Islamic law of inheritance has not been observed; or such as were mortgaged by the poor and the big feudalist has included as part of his own property. Besides, the crop-sharing ratio, fair and just, should also have been fixed and those conditions declared as punishable crime which were imposed, orally or in practice, on the peasants and on account of which these wretches were forced to a life of slavery. The middlemen should also have been eliminated so as to enable the peasants to reap the full benefits of their crops.

Briefly, so intricate are the defects of our agricultural system, and it is not possible to resolve them by merely imposing a maximum limit of 150 acres. The fact is that limiting ownership is a way by which the real problems of the agricultural sector cannot possibly be resolved. The doors still remain open for the black- marketers and other frauds. This has been our experience of the limitation imposed in 1959 and can be no better now.

Moreover, the special allowances made of 15,000 units for all land owners and of 3000 units for those who had installed tube- wells or purchased tractors before December 1971, render the reform thoroughly meaningless. Besides, the ownership limit is based on individuals and not families. This allows many loopholes and there still are landlords each in possession of thousands of acres.

For such reasons, Islam has not stipulated any limits on land ownership but based its order on permissibility and impermissibility, and made justice free and accessible. Seen pragmatically, this is the only way of dealing with or preventing oppression and cruelty. Irrespective of its size, all impermissibly owned land must be seized and ownership of that possessed by legitimate means strictly protected.

Similarly, a landlord who is not guilty of oppressing his peasant in any way is outside the pale of Islamic censure or punishment, however much land he may own, but he who by word of mouth or in practice is oppressive or holds the peasant as unequal in mutual agreements, perhaps, reducing him to a vassal state, or does not give sufficient remuneration for his labor, is guilty and liable to punishment irrespective of how little he may possess.

Therefore, the rights of the peasantry cannot be made secure unless the following measures are adopted:

Without placing any limits on the ownership, all lands impermissibly held should be taken away and transferred to their rightful owners; and, if the rightful owners cannot be traced, they should be distributed among the landless.

The Islamic Laws of inheritance should be strictly enforced, and byelaws framed according to the Shariah in respect of "bringing dead land to life".

All lands mortgaged with the landlords should be seized and returned to the borrowers.

Rules for crop sharing should be such as will ensure putting an end to concentration of wealth and bringing about a balanced economy.

In respect of conditions for crop sharing, those that are illegitimate should be made punishable and steps should be taken to give equality to both the parties.

Middlemen, brokers and such, should be eliminated or their working so modified that the peasant may be able to sell his produce without pressure of any kind.

Banks operating without charging interest on loans should be established to enable the peasants to purchase agricultural implements on easy installments.

Above all, special courts of justice with wide easily accessible to the peasants should be set up. powers and today, the greatest difficulty faced by the poor is that justice is not available to them. It is easier for them to be patient over their condition, howsoever cruel, than to run about for years to courts of law wasting their time and money. Especially when the opposing party happens to be a big and influential feudalist, a poor and oppressed man cannot even have the courage to approach a law-court.

If justice cannot be made available to the poor and oppressed, the best of laws can do nothing to help them. Therefore, it is necessary to attend to this matter first.

We cannot go into greater detail here. Our purpose is to point out that the defects in our present agricultural system cannot be removed except by way of Islam and for this purpose we shall have to work from different angles and with the cooperation of expert jurists, agriculturists and intellectuals.

President Bhutto announcing the land reforms said:

> *Should the limitation of ownership be based on the basis of family or on the basis of individuals"; the issue was considered thoroughly. As this was an issue of Islamic jurisprudence, we restored to the eminent religious scholars and jurists for an advice thereof. The conclusion that emerged that as Islam acknowledges the rights of individual and does not recommend the system of family ownership, hence, being a Muslim, we cannot even imagine of a scheme which is in contravention to Islamic trends. Therefore, this limitation has been imposed on the basis of individuals and not on this basis of family".*
>
> (DAWN 3 March 1972)

The words, "We cannot even think of any scheme that is opposed to Islam.", are worthy of appreciation. But we are unable to imagine who those authorities are that, instead of stipulating in full all the relevant Islamic requirements, have simply used Islam to open a backdoor for the feudalists to wriggle out of the limitation law.

Interest and Banking

Answer to a Questionnaire By Mufti Muhammed Shafi:

Recently, the Council of Islamic ideology issued a questionnaire on the subject of Riba. The answers given by Mufti Muhammed Shafi are given below: -

Question-1:

(a) What is the concept of Riba in the light of the Quran and Sunnah, and before Islam, what was understood by Riba? Does. Takhsisa imply the doubling or tripling of the principal money, or does it include only simple and compound interest?

Answer:

The meaning of the word Riba as enunciated by the Quran is unambiguous. According to the Quran, the Sunnah, the practice of the Companions and as understood generally by the ummah, any increment above whatever is loaned out is Riba, whether it be simple interest or compound. Many books and essays have been written by a number of writers on the subject. I too have written an article titled Masla e Sood published in a journal which is being included here. Some points may be clarified:

The Quran states in some detail:

"O you who believe, fear Allah and give up whatever is yet due as Riba, if you are indeed believers.

These words include every amount of Riba. Further, it is added:

"And if you repent, your principal is yours. Do not oppress others, and you will not be oppressed.

In this context, repentance means that the lender must not demand any extra above his principal; and the words "oppress not and you will not be oppressed", imply that any excess, however, small, is forbidden.

In another place, (Surah 3.130) the words are: -

"Do not devour Riba multiplying it over and over again."

This is not a juristic condition, but a warning about the worst form of Riba, similar to the command,

"Do not sell My Verses for a small price,"

which does not imply that though "My Verses" must not be sold for a small price they may be sold for a high price. The words are intended only to identify the sin. The words "over and over again" identify the enormity otherwise, the command in Surah e Baqar would not have stated that on repentance only the principal shall be due to the lender.

Several times has the Prophet clarified that every amount above the principal is Riba. Imam Shafi and Imam Ibn Hatim quote the Prophet's words:

"Attention! All the Riba that was due in the days of Ignorance has been ended. Do not oppress and you will not be oppressed. First of all, the Riba due to Abbas Ibn Muttalib is being written off in the full amount, now and here" (Commentary Ibn Kathir)

Explaining the meaning of the word, the Prophet said,

"Every loan given to pull in profit is Riba"

(Al Jama- a bil Saghir li- yasooti, ref. Harith b. Abi Asama Vol. 1 p.94, Tradition No. 6336)

Accordingly, the Companions always understood Riba to mean any increment, however, small or great, above the principal. Fadlata bin Obayd, a well-known Companion, defines Riba as "any profit on a loan is among the forms of Riba", Kulla qaradun jarra munfaata hua wajha mun wajuhu el Riba. (Alsunanul Kubra Baihaqi vol. 5 p.350).) Bukhari has quoted Abdullah b. Omer as saying,

"There is no harm in lending money for a fixed period even if the borrower returns the loan with better quality coins, provided this (returning with better coins) is not included among the terms of the loan."

(Sahih Bukhari Vol.1 p.323)

It is clear that it will be Riba if the return with better quality coins is included among the terms of the agreement.

Abu Huraira says,

"I was advised by Abdullah b. Salam, 'You are living in a region where Riba is common practice, so if anyone has to return you any loan and he gives you a load of hay or barley as a gift, do not accept it because it will be Riba."

(Sahih Bukhari Vol.1 p.538)

Qutada b. Da- amata el Doosi comments on the words,

"If you repent, the principal is yours.......", "If a man owes you some money, the Quran permits you to take the principal back but does not permit you any amount above it."

The various lexicons similarly define the word. Zujaja's dictionary defines the word, "Every loan by means of which more money is received." (Taj ul Uroos). Lisan ul Arab also defines Riba in the same words. All the ulema and Muslim jurists give the same meaning to the word. Abu Bakar Hassass defines Riba as prevalent during the Times of Ignorance, "A loan repayable within a fixed time with an agreed increment above the loan.

There is no vagueness or doubt in these definitions, making it quite clear that whatever excess on a loan is taken or given by agreement is Riba. No distinction is made between simple and compound interest. This is the command of the Quran and Sunnah, and this is the ummah's decisive acceptance. No loophole is left for any other interpretation.

Question-1:

(b) Because of the progress and changes taking place after the advent of Islam, can a new interpretation be given to Riba?

Answer: To give a brief, concise answer, "by no means". Reinterpreting what has already been interpreted by the Quran and the Traditions, and has always been conceded unanimously by the ummah, would be plain tampering. Doing so would mean that no command of the Quran or Sunnah should eventually be left unaltered. If out of consideration for the changing times Riba is given a modified meaning, new interpretations may likewise be made for strong drink, adultery and even kufr and shirk, denial and associating partners with God. What Islamic requirements can then be secured?

For commands permitted to be modified according to the exigencies of the times, the Quran and Sunnah have laid down rules of guidance but where no such indication is given the commands are absolute and cannot be subjected to any modification whatsoever. Their execution must be unvarying too. If any change in respect of Riba were permissible, the Quran would not devote two whole sections (ruku) to the subject. Holding on to Riba is equated with war against Allah and His Prophet. The Prophet warns that the worst of punishments await the practitioners of Riba, while not the slightest indication is found anywhere in the Quran that its implications may be changed at any time. Instead, the relevant statement we find in the Traditions is the Prophet's declaration, "A time will come when there will be none left who has not consumed Riba, and he who may not have consumed Riba, the dust of it will certainly reach him."

(Abu Dawood and Ibn Maja)

And further:

"When the Last Day nears, Riba, strong drink and adultery will be quite common.

That is, the Prophet warns of the day when it will be difficult to keep away from Riba or its "dust", yet he declares Riba to be impermissible.

Today, according to the Prophecy quoted, we see the widespread prevalence of Riba. Though usury is no longer likely, blank-interest remains as one form of Riba the effects of which extend to everyone, directly or indirectly.

Question 2:

Is trade based on interest permissible between two Muslim states or one Muslim and the other non-Muslim?

Answer: Such trade among Muslim states is not permissible but, according to some jurists, fuqaha, with a non-Muslim state, it may be allowed, not because interest is valid but that property belonging to non-Muslims living in a non-Muslim country, Dar ul Harb, is legitimate and may be taken by their permission, whatever name they may give it. Therefore, in conditions beyond Muslim control, the trade is legitimate.

Question 3:

Does interest on loans issued by the government fall in the category of Riba?

Answer: There is no doubt that it is Riba. Riba that is impermissible for a Muslim individually is also impermissible for the government.

Question 4:

In your opinion, is interest-free banking possible? If so, on what premises?

Answer: There is no doubt that non-interest banking is possible. The details are beyond the scope of this Questionnaire, but a general outline may be given here. The best way to get on with this task would be to convene a conference of Muslim jurists and economic experts to draw up a workable plan, instead of wasting time on the permissibility or impermissibility of interest.

The outline includes:

Working on the principles of profit-sharing and Mudarbah. This would entail that deposits made in the bank will be of two categories; loans payable on demand (Current Accounts) and Fixed Deposits for Mudarbah. Savings Accounts will be included in the Current Accounts.

All deposits made in the bank as payable on demand, current accounts, will be loans, according to fiqh law, and drawable at any time by cheque, but no profit will be given to the depositor, as the practice already is. Profits, however, will be given in proportion to the amount of deposits made under Mudarbah which may be for any period between three and twelve months. In other words, whatever the ratio of such deposit to the bank's invested money, the same will be the ratio of the depositor's profit to the profit the bank makes.

Of the deposits under Current or Mudarbah Accounts the bank, after keeping back some money in reserve, may give a part of the deposit to the depositor-businessman on the basis of profit sharing or Mudarbah to invest in business and the depositor- businessman will return the principal together with an agreed proportion of his total profits to the bank. The bank will then distribute the total of the amount so collected among its co-sharers and account holders according to their pre-arranged shares.

Side by side, the bank will continue with its prevalent services, such as locker facilities, issuing traveler's cheques, bank drafts, letters of credit, brokerage, business advice and such on payment for its work.

These are but broad hints for changing over to interest-free banking. There are several books where the subject is discussed in detail. Banking experts have been consulted and they agree on the feasibility of the plan. An organization should be set up further to deliberate and give it practical shape.

Question 5:

Can any distinction be made in the light of Islamic commands, between private and government banking vis a vis the realization of interest money in return for services rendered by the bank?

Answer: According to Islam, there is no difference between private and government banking. What is permissible for the one is permissible for the other, and interest-bearing transactions are impermissible for both.

Question 6:

Can government banking or that of any organization under its supervision be declared the property of an absentee owner. If so, what will be the exact position of such an organization in the light of Islam?

Answer: Banks established by the government are the government's property. The question of absentee ownership does not arise in respect of them.

Question 7:

(a): According to Islam, can capital be looked upon as an agent of production; and would it be permissible to give any compensation for its use?

(b): If so, does Islam stipulate any share for the capital in the distribution of profits?

Answer: This is a polemic question not touched upon by the Quran, but the Quran does look upon capital as an agent of production. In modern economics as well as according to the Shariah, real capital consists of: -

a): Circulating capital, such as money, which produces nothing until it is invested; and;

b): fixed capital, such as machinery. Compensation of the first is profit and of the second rent.

A detailed account of this subject is given in my essay, "Distribution of Wealth in Islam", a copy of which is attached hereto.

Question 8:

(a): In your opinion, is it possible to do business within the country and with other countries without the services rendered by the bank and without interest bearing transactions?

(b): If your answer is in the negative, can you suggest alternatives that are in keeping with Islam?

Answer: Yes, it is possible. It has already been stated that the remuneration a bank takes for its services is permissible. But interest is impermissible. The alternative is given in the answer to Question No.4.

Question 9:

Can insurance be conducted without interest?

Answer: Yes. The collected sums of money should be invested in trading (according to Shariah Mudarbah principles), and instead of interest, the profit should be distributed as under banking.

Insurance should be on cooperative lines. If the policy holder agree, a part of the total profits, a half, a third or a fourth, may be kept in reserve to be spent as need arises on accident cases, etc. according to the rules.

This assistance will be available only for those who are shareholders in the company and are bound by the relevant agreement. Already such stipulations are valid in trusts, for example trusts for one's children, Waqf ul-al-Aulad.

The full amount of one's principal money together with the profit will be payable to him, (except in case of loss to the company). The reserve fund of the cooperative will be a trust, the benefit of which will accrue also to the founder of the trust, just as one may benefit by a hospital founded by him or be buried in a graveyard donated by him as a trust.

Suitable rules should be made for assistance to accident for the usual type of accidents a fixed amount should be set cases. aside for the help of the poor; and for accidents not usually looked upon as such, for example death caused by disease. Some financial assistance may be given to the heirs in the event of a normally healthy man dying before he is sixty years of age; this age being looked upon as the normal life span. The present Insurance system of medically determining normal health may be continued.

If the insured discontinues paying his installments, the amount already paid by him must not be confiscated, because it is impermissible in Islam to do so. To prevent the Company from undergoing any loss, one of the conditions laid down may be that the paid in money will not be refundable before the expiry of five or more years. The share of the insured person in the profits may also be reduced. All such matters may be settled by the Company as they do not affect the permissibility or impermissibility of the transactions.

This is only a brief, proposed plan. The views of other parties should be invited for consideration, and modifications, alterations and additions may be made, keeping within the Shariah.

Question 12:

Is the profit paid on Savings Accounts and Provident Fund included in Riba?[6]

Answer: There is no doubt that the profit paid on Savings Account is Riba, as already explained in the definition of the word given in the answer to Question No.1. As for Provident Funds, the best way to avoid the "dust" of Riha would be to invest the money in trade by Mudarbah or co-sharing and distribute the profits in proportion to the share of each beneficiary. However, the present system of giving as fixed "interest" part of the profits earned by investing the Provident Fund money in business is quite valid, as it does not fall within the definition of Riba. The reason is that the part of the employee's salary held back by the employer does not belong to the employee and has not yet come into his possession but is continuing in the ownership of the employer. Now, the extra that the employer, government or whatever organization, makes with the Provident Fund is with its own money, not with that of its employee. If the employer gives the employee a part of the extra it is a reward, and it is permissible for the employee to accept the reward. Details of this subject have been published in this writer's pamphlet Provident Fund, and the other ulema have approved of it. A copy of the pamphlet is attached hereto.

---

[6] For convenience Question No. 12 is being taken before No. 11.

Question 11:

(a): Is the money that an employee borrows from his Provident Fund and is later deposited in the same Fund, Riba?

Answer: In line with the explanation given above, this is neither a loan nor a subject of "interest", from the Shariah point of view. It is not a loan because the employee has not asked for anything except a part of the loan which the employer already owes him and which the employee has every right to demand. And the amount, which is deducted from the salary in the name of "borrowed money and interest", is not paying back a loan but only a deduction similarly to the deduction that was normally being made. The only difference is that the amount now deducted will be greater for the reason that it will also be returned to the employee.

(b): What will be the position if the employee increases his Provident Fund by adding his own money to it?

Answer: This will make no difference because the extra money added to his own Fund is also a kind of reward on his behalf.

Question 13:

Is the money given as a reward on Savings Accounts or Prize Bonds included in the definition of Riba?

Answer: Interest is charged on prize bonds, and the amount thus collected is paid to one purchaser of the bond, selected by lottery, instead of all the purchasers. This makes no difference. The money given as a prize is definitely interest, and therefore, Riba. However, in consultation with men of learning, suitable alterations can be made in the present system so as to render it free of Riba.

Interest paid on Savings Accounts, as said repeatedly before, is pure Riba. Money given on such Accounts as a prize is by agreement, Upd e Riba, which it is not permissible for anyone to accept.

Question 14:

Under Islamic Law, is it permissible to discriminate between loans taken for business and those taken for other purposes when interest is chargeable on the former but not on the latter?

Answer: As said before, Riba is every agreed extra amount that is charged or taken on a loan. The purpose for which the loan is given or taken makes no difference. If the lender lends the money with the intention of merely helping the borrower, it is necessary for him to forego any profit, but if his motive is to profit by lending the money, he shall have to abide by the normal principles of business, or by co- sharing the profit as well as the loss, whichever occurs. Islam allows no alternative. The lender is not permitted to make the profit and his principal secure in all circumstances while the prospects of the other party, the borrower, remain uncertain.

Question 10:

Does the Islamic economic order encourage savings for the purpose of creating national wealth?

Question 15:

If Riba interest is totally eliminated what motivation does Islam provide for stimulating people to live according to a planned budget and be frugal and thrifty.

Answer: Both these questions are really the same. If banks and insurance companies are run on principles of co-sharing and Mudarbah, the clients will earn a greater profit than through interest because they will be co-sharers of the whole business. What can be a more encouraging system for national savings?

This leaves only the Savings Account because in an interest- free system it gets neither profit nor interest. But according to economic experts, the nominal rate of interest for Savings Accounts is not a pressing incentive for savings. The real cause of savings is frugality. No substantial loss is incurred to this item by not paying interest on Savings Accounts. Besides, the minimum period for Fixed Accounts can be reduced to three months or one year to attract those who wish to save as well as earn a profit.

Question 16:

In modern economics theory the meanings of "interest" actually payable on loans is different from the "rate of interest". For instance, for the completion of development plans the economic experts work on an hypothetical interest rate, which indicates insufficiency of capital. Can this method be used for a practical economics blueprint, whether interest is actually paid or not?

Answer: The question is not clear; however, if the idea is whether decisions can be made in matters of development planning etc., on the basis of assumed rates of interest, the answer is that such a need can arise only where interest is actually practiced. If the economy is conducted wholly without interest, there can be no need for assuming a rate of interest.

(Mufti Muhammed Shafi - End 107)

Remembrance and thought Interest-free Counters.

All Glory and Praise are to Him Who gave existence to the manufactory of this world, And Blessings be on His Last Prophet who proclaimed His Truth!

The government has announced that interest-free Banking will be conducted from the 1st of January 1981, and related counters have already been opened. We are told that this is the first step towards interest-free banking, and gradually the whole banking system will be altered to this end.

To get rid of such an accursed institution as "interest" is among the most important of government duties. The day our economy is relieved of this satanic cycle will be one of great blessings not only for Pakistan but all humanity!

The present government has announced its determination repeatedly that it wants to reconstruct the national economy on interest-free foundations. Muslims have welcomed this announcement made as it is in an atmosphere where attempts are being made to sanctify bank-interest and accounts are being opened at these counters.

Personally, we have been opposed to the running of interest and interest-free counters side by side, but since the interest-free counters have been inaugurated, we should try to make them successful. They are the outcome of a long period of wishing and effort and waiting for third of a century. We thought that whatever the method, the very commencement of interest-free banking is a propitious step cooperating with which is itself a blessing. Therefore, we studied the scheme with high emotions and a sense of participation, but it is a great pity, that after going through the details of the working of these counters, our emotions have chilled to a great extent.

Since January 1981 we have been receiving letters from various quarters asking us whether "interest" has really been eliminated by the opening of these counters, and whether a Muslim may now, without any fear, open an account at these counters.

Reflecting deeper in order to reply to such questions we discovered that the mind long accustomed to "interest" is not prepared to put an end to it so easily and would like to continue the old practice by polishing it up with attractive ingredients. Muslims will, therefore, have to wait for some time longer and make further efforts to topple this wall, --- which is already tottering and is bound ultimately to collapse.

As the Muslims and even the ulema have not yet received all the details of the scheme, we shall comment only on the material we have received so far to enable the government and the public as well as the ulema to carve out a path of action.

How are banks to be run on interest-free lines and what in place of interest will be the base for the economy?

The subject has been under the consideration of several individuals and organizations in the world of Islam and a great deal of work has already been done on it. Two points emerge as common to these deliberations: one, distribution of both profits and loss, that is, co-sharing and Mudarbah; and two, free loans, qurd e hasana. This means that banking shall have to be conducted wholly on these two premises. Of course, there are other functions, which the banks have to perform and are not related to free loans or Mudarbah. Proposals have been advanced by some people in connection with these functions, but they cannot be made a permanent or basic feature of banking and can be looked upon only as exceptional or temporary and transitory. The scholarly and detailed work that has so far come, at least to my knowledge, is the report prepared by the Council of Islamic Ideology with the assistance of the ulema and economics experts.

The gist of this report too is the same: that banking should be done on profit and loss sharing basis, and most of the bank's work should be conducted on co-sharing and Mudarbah lines. But where this cannot be done, alternative methods have been proposed to be used as and when the need arises. Among these alternatives is what is called "Mark Up" (bai muajjal).

This may be understood briefly by the following example.

For instances, a man wants to buy a tractor and he approaches a bank for a loan. Here partnership or Mudarbah is not applicable because the borrower requires the tractor for his personal use, cultivating his field, and not for business. The ideal thing for the bank to do would be to give the man a free loan, but for want of sufficient capital at its disposal the bank cannot do this. As an alternative, the bank may buy the tractor and transfer it immediately to the man but at the bank's own price to be paid later, the price will include a profit or labor charges as "Mark Up". (The transaction is bai muajjal).

This is by no means an ideal way to avert interest, but because the bank sells the tractor after bringing it to its ownership, possession and risk, the profit it charges is not interest. Islamic jurists have permitted such transaction under certain conditions. Therefore, the Council Report makes certain allowances until better alternatives come up before the bank. But this does not mean that the whole banking structure may be rebuilt on Markup. Thus the Council's Report lays down certain limits where it states the "delayed payment" method among several alternatives to interest bearing transactions. The words of the Introduction to the Report are:

"The Council wishes to make it clear at the very beginning that in the Islamic economic order the alternative to interest is co- sharing profit and loss or free loans for providing capital. Although many of the proposals made here are based on profit-and-loss shares, there are others, which relate to such procedures as patta dari, ownership, rent, Mark Up, using capital by auctioneering. The alternatives as presented here are purged of interest, they are only secondary alternative solutions in the ideal Islamic economics. There is also the danger that these methods may be used as back doors to reintroduce interest-bearing transactions and the consequent evils. It is, therefore, necessary that these methods should be used with great hesitation and only where other alternatives cannot be thought of. They should never, never be allowed to assume that traditional use of capital."

And it is repeated in connection with the details of Mark Up:

"Although according to Islamic shariah it is permissible to employ this mode, it will be unwise to use it in all cases without discrimination, because it will be taking a great risk for the opening of back- doors for interest bearing transactions. Therefore, only such safe channels should be used as make any resort to this method necessary, where other alternatives do not exist. "

(Report of the Islamic Council of Ideology Pages 13 & 17).

In this context, we find the scheme implemented since January I as quite the opposite. Not only has Mark Up been made the basis of all business at the "non-interest" counter, none of the conditions of the working of Markup, which would make it justifiable according to fiqh, have been observed. We find the following serious defects in the scheme:

Business by delayed payment is permissible only if the commodity sold is in the actual possession of the seller. It is a well- known Islamic principle that no one may sell a thing which is not in his possession and for which he takes no risk. The scheme under review mentions no such condition of the bank. It goes so far as to allow the bank not to sell a commodity, for example rice, to its client, but only to give him the market price of it to enable him to purchase it. The words of the scheme are:

"It will be assumed that the commodities for which the bank provides the money have been purchased by the bank in return for the money and has sold them within ninety days (to the one who came to the bank to get the money). "

(State Bank News Jan. 1, 1981 p.9)

How and when a commodity comes to the bank's possession and ownership is not mentioned here. How can it be understood that a commodity one wants to buy has been purchased by the bank and then sold by it? Mere writing on the paper cannot be equated with the actual fulfillment of the condition. At the most what can be done is that the bank should appoint its customer as its agent and then, after the commodity comes into this agent's possession, in his capacity as the bank's agent, the bank may sell it to him. This procedure should be clearly written down and also that until the commodity comes into his possession, the money provided by the bank to the agent will not be a loan but held in trust by him.

No such words are found in the scheme. What is stated is that on March 28 it will be understood that whatever moneys the banks had given their clients previous to March 28 have been returned to the banks together with the interest on that date, and, then, on the same day, the banks have given the same money back to their clients on Mark Up.; and that it will be assumed that the commodities for the purchase of which the banks had provided the loan have been purchased by them and sold by them on the basis of mark Up. We fail to appreciate the logic of this mode of working.

It is clear that "delayed payment" is used here only for its name, and moreover even the name is renounced and provided money is called an Advance Loan and the word used is "lend".

(State Bank News Jan. 1, 1981, p.7)

There is another very serious defect in this scheme. It is necessary that for "delayed payment", the price should be settled at the time the transaction is made and also the time when the price will be paid. Should the buyer not pay up on the agreed date, he may be sued accordingly to the law, but the shariah provides no justification for increasing the price because this would be equal to charging an interest. No such clarification is made in the scheme; rather the principle has been clearly violated in some matters. For instance, it is stated that the Mark Up for the first 20 days on the money provided by a bank for import bills shall be .78 per cent, and if the dues are not paid up within 20 days, there will be an increase of .58 per cent; and if not paid within 34 days, there will be a further increase of .62 per cent; and if not paid within 48 days, an increase of.79 per cent will be charged every 15 days!

If this is not charging interest, what is it? Merely to name interest as Mark Up does not modify the reality of the "interest".

So, far the increase in the Mark Up rates has been stated only in respect of import bills, but what is there to stop the same being applied to other bank transactions?

The method proposed for cashing hundis and bills of exchange is no different form, what is current already, except that the word Discount has been replaced with the term "Mark down", although the Report of the Council of Islamic Ideology makes definite proposals for cashing hundis according to Islamic principles.

Even if these difficulties were removed, the fact would still remain the Mark Up instead of co-sharing and Mudarbah has been made the basis of banking transactions. According to the State Bank News of January 1, 1981, it has been decided that moneys deposited at the interest-free counters will be used under seven different heads of which only one relates to co-sharing and Mudarbah and the remaining six to Mark Up, or Mark Down. Besides, no new plan has been drawn up for using the money, under Mudarbah and co- sharing, but that it will be used for purchasing company shares, NIT Units and Party Term Certificates or invested in those transactions of the Investment Corporation of Pakistan or Bankers' Equity which are conducted on principles of co-sharing of profit and loss.

The result of this can only be to invest all the moneys of the interest-free counters in those bodies which are already doing business on Mudarbah or profit and loss basis, and not for widening the circle of co-sharing and Mudarbah, under which only marginal business will be done. This means that banking will not be Islamised but will continue as it has always been.

The question that may fairly be asked here is, if "delayed payment" is permissible under the Shariah, why should banking not be conducted wholly according to the Shariah, and why should stress not be laid on partnership and Mudarbah?

The reason is that although the "delayed payment", in which the price is increased because of the loan involved may not be "interest" in the technical sense of the word, yet the "interest" system is liable to encouragement. Therefore, this is not a desirable way.

To make it the basis of banking is not right for the following reasons:

There are differences of opinion among the Islamic jurists over the permissibility of increasing the price when a thing is sold on deferred payment. A majority of them look upon it as permissible while the others believe that although this is not "interest" in the legal sense, it does resemble interest, a selfish motive is evident, and they hold it as impermissible. One of them is Qazi Khan a Hanafi alim. Therefore, when here are differences of opinion among the jurists and the resemblance is evident, it can be availed of at times of great emergency, but not for building up a whole structure of billions of capitals for use as a common routine.

Banks by themselves are not commercial houses, but only provide the capital for trade, industry and agriculture. It is quite different for a business organization to adopt the "deferred payment" system, but if a bank, which is neither a commercial house nor possesses commercial goods, adopts the "deferred payment" routine, it can be only as paperwork with no reality behind it, the whole motive being to use it as an excuse for avoiding the restrictions on "interest".

When we talk of interest-free banking and running banks on Islamic principles, we certainly do not mean that the present system may be altered very slightly and the main work done as customary, but that the entire order should be changed so as to adapt it to Islamic principles, the effects of which should spread over the social distribution of wealth.

The concept of capital investment in Islam is that the investor should either not require a profit or, if profit is desired, the risk of loss should also be shared. This is a basic Islamic principle which shall have to be secured for interest-free banking but is rendered inapplicable if nearly all the bank business is to be conducted on Mark Up basis.

Are we to go about trying to make the world believe that we clamoured against the defects of the current banking system only that Mark Up should replace the "interest"? Can Mark Up be used as a way out for getting rid of even a fraction of the defects of wealth distribution? If not, and it certainly cannot be used as such ---, what kind of a picture of Islamic capital investment are we presenting before the world?

Our jurists have, therefore, decided that for resolving a legal difficulty in one or two cases, a shariah way out may be sought but such escape doors cannot be used to destroy the objectives of the Shariah.

The fact is that the kind of capital invest Islam requires cannot be achieved by the cosmetics of Mark Up. To this end we need revolutionary thinking, not superficial polishing. Business organizations shall have to be compelled to conduct their business along co-sharing or Mudarbah lines; they shall have to change their system of keeping accounts; the tax laws, especially income-tax laws, shall have to be modified so that instead of being virtual invitations to dishonesty and corruption, they inspire trust and emotions of serving the society and country. And most of all, that mentality shall have to be changed which demands a profit on every penny without taking the least risk of loss.

We, therefore, request our government that since they have made up their minds to rid the national economy of "interest" do not doubt their motives we and they are also ready to take practical steps to the end, they should not go about it half-heartedly, because in such matters half-heartedness can be very dangerous, but take those steps with full courage and single-mindedness which are necessary for such a tremendous and pious work. So far it is only the beginning of interest-free counters when it is comparatively easy to improve. With the lapse of time, complications are bound to creep in. We suggest that the following should be done with immediate effect:

Interest-free business should be conducted on profit and loss sharing instead of Mark Up.

Shariah conditions should be fulfilled where Mark Up is indispensable. First, delayed or deferred payment should not entail any price-increase because the Shariah does not permit this. Next, it must be ascertained that goods sold under Mark Up must actually be in the bank's possession.

Mark Down system should be replaced by that which has been proposed by the Council of Islamic Ideology.

Investors at the non-interest counters have not been told what share of the profits theirs will be. That is, it is not clear what ratio of its profit the bank will keep for itself and what it will give its investors. Instead, it has been stated that the distribution of the profits shall be at the bank's discretion. All this is not in accordance with the Shariah. When negotiations are being made with the investor for co-sharing profit and loss the proportion of his share and that of the bank in the profits should be clearly stated at the same time, otherwise, according to the Shariah, the validity of the transaction will be rendered doubtful.

The question now remains, what will be the Shariah position of the profits for those whose accounts have been opened at the "non-interest" counters? And whether those people on whom Allah has bestowed the will to save themselves from "interest", should be in future open their accounts at these counters or not.

There are three parts to the details of the "non-interest" counter transactions.

The first part is unambiguously valid. The profits on money invested in the non-preferential shares of public companies or purchase of NIT Units or in some other business run on the basis of co-sharing of profit and loss or Mudarbah will be permissible in Shariah law.

The second part is impermissible. The system of the increase in Mark Up rate or Price increase on import bills, when payment is not made on stipulated time, is definitely invalid by the Shariah, and so too the profits derived from such transactions. Similarly, the profits derived from discount in the name of Mark Down on internal bills will also be impermissible.

The third part is vague. The method stated for Mark Up in respect of bills other than import is not clearly stated. The profits derived here will be invalid. Any increase of the Mark Up rate in case of delay in payment and the goods sold by the bank under Mark Up without their coming in its possession, both will be invalid.

This analysis shows that for the present the transactions of the "non-interest counters" are hybrid mixtures of the permissible and impermissible and some are ambiguous. Therefore, until these defects are removed it will not be proper for Muslims to involve themselves in such traffic.

Now we may ask who those worthies are that are responsible for deceiving the Muslims by contriving this un-Islamic Plan in the name of "interest-free banking". When the government has announced time and again that it is bound by its intention to purge the national economy of "interest", and the Council of Islamic Ideology, too, with its panel, after a whole year of laborious work, has submitted a detailed report which has also been published, who has given whom the right to throw away this report and draw up a plan which is opposed to the shariah commands and which having been labelled as "Interest-free banking", amounts to a fraud on the Muslims?

We appeal to President General Muhammed Zia ul Haq to give this matter his immediate attention and not only have the errors rectified, but also order an investigation to find out who are responsible for them, and who those elements are that are constantly obstructing every step taken to implement the Islamic social order. We have been patient with their manipulating long enough; it is high time that notice was taken, and the nation relieved of them before the masses lose their patience, otherwise the results can only be disastrous not only for the country but also for the government.

May Allah grant those in power the will and ability to purge this new order of its un-Islamic content so that Muslims may devote themselves totally and with single-minded purpose to participate in making interest-free banking a success!

Finally, we request the ulema, especially those of vision in juristic matters, to study carefully the report of the Council of Islamic Ideology, analyze it thoroughly and point out the weaknesses. The report is by no means the last word. The purpose of publishing it is to improve it as far as possible. Suggestions are cordially invited so that it may be completed, and the task of its implementation made easy.

Muhammed Taqi Usmani 18 Rabi I, 1401 AH

Savings week and Government's Revenue Schemes

Glory Be to him who gave existence to this world And Blessings and peace be on his last Prophet who held high the banner of truth!

The government has announced the observance of a savings week throughout the country commencing the 15th. Of May to the 20th. In his message the President said that the motive for the Savings Week was to make us realize that our moral responsibility was to save a part of our income for investing it in national schemes.

He said that the economic progress of country depended upon capital investment in development plans and the planning depended upon the availability of funds. That is why the savings of an individual contribute to the nation's economic progress. It is an acknowledged truth that dependence on foreign aid is reduced in proportion to the extent we exploit our country's resources. Therefore, every citizen should put himself on oath that he will save a part of his income for national savings schemes.

The Revenue Minister, Ghulam Ishaq Khan, has also said in his message that no country can achieve its desired objectives without hard labor and frugality. In our country, the savings rate was far less than that in other countries, on account of which we are obliged to seek foreign assistance to meet our capital requirements. That is why it is the Islamic duty of every one of us and our patriotic obligation to live simple lives and save whatever little or much we can. He appealed to Pakistani nationals living abroad to make the Savings Week a success by investing in the various national savings schemes.

(Jung 15 May 1982)

Previous governments too have made similar appeals to the public for simple, frugal living and savings from income, but the appeal made by the present authorities is particularly noteworthy because they also profess to implement the Islamic Shariah. Its constant announcements cannot be hidden from anyone that it is doing its best to Islamise every department of life, social, economic, legal or political. This is the first item on the list of its priorities, and it has already taken some steps in this direction. Hence the revenue minister has referred in respect of the public's "Islamic Duty" to save and live frugally and invest in the National Savings Schemes.

A sizeable volume is required to state the Islamic teachings and commands on the subject of "savings", but because there are many misunderstandings about it and the subject is not under our consideration, we shall confine ourselves to some relevant details here.

There cannot be two opinions in respect of importance of "savings", avoiding extravagance and investing in national constructive works. But there are certain religious and practical aspects, which must be kept in view because without them the declared objectives cannot be achieved. The appeal for investing in the National Savings Schemes as an Islamic duty is quite amusing.

To advocate savings, frugality, and simple living will remain no more than a sermon of hollow words as long as government does not create the right environment by its economic policies and setting an example by its own way of life. When the common man sees the high-ups, the ministers and government officers, and their standard of living, he finds not even a shadow of simplicity anywhere. Luxury goods and luxury living are the result of extravagant government policies. There is an ever-increasing race for possession of television sets, VCRs, air-conditioners, refrigerators and such luxury items. Without them everyone feels deprived and oppressed and this feeling of deprivation makes one acquire the money for them by any means, legitimate or not. The great majority of people comprises those who find it difficult to meet the expenses of their daily necessities; and if they do have some money to spare, it is spent on some luxury item or another. In these conditions, how can there be any money left over for "savings".

It is perfectly true that to live with simplicity is an Islamic duty, and correct also that to strive for the country's economic development is a patriotic demand, but is it not the government's Islamic duty to provide the Muslims with such ways and means as will enable them to devote their savings to national prosperity without getting them involved in the curse that "interest" is.

If anyone wishes to live in simplicity and devote his savings to government's savings schemes, what alternative is there open to him except that he participates in the government's "interest" schemes? Therefore, the government's advice that people should save is no more than asking them to participate in interest-bearing transactions.

The present government may be congratulated for its acknowledgment of the impermissibility of "interest" and the defects thereof. It has also announced its intention to purge the national economy of "interest" and establish an interest free revenue department, whereas the former governments hesitated to acknowledge the illegitimacy and sometimes have even tried to prove that "interest" is not forbidden in Islam. However, it is very disappointing that the present government has been very slow and indifferent to taking practical steps in the matter.

In 1979, the government had announced that it would purge three of its organizations, the NIT, ICP Mutual Fund, and the House Building Finance Corporation, of "interest". It was thought at the time that this was the beginning, and gradually every revenue department would be similarly relieved, but three years have passed since, and no steps have been taken in the promised direction, while it is often heard that these departments are fully engrossed in interest- bearing commerce.

Also, no action has yet been taken on the Report prepared by a distinguished body of some ulema and economics and banking experts under the supervision of the Council of Islamic Ideology despite a passage of two years since it was published. During this time, it was also announced on behalf of the government that co- sharing profit and loss accounts had been inaugurated in the banks as a preliminary to interest-free banking, but, as we wrote in al Balagh, the actual working of these accounts were not in accordance with the Shariah and also contravene the Council's Report, attention to which has been drawn by the Chairman. In spite of all this, those accounts have been operating as usual. They have been given the name of interest free banking and people are getting involved in this anti Shariah commerce believing that it is according to Shariah. Even those organizations, which are bound to invest their capital in non-interest commerce, do not hesitate resorting to those Accounts. We have been informed that the NIT and ICP have deposited some of their funds in such accounts.

We have also been informed that the government faces some difficulties in regard to implementing the Council's Report. If that is so, the best way would have been for representatives of the Council, the Revenue Department and related organizations to sit together for resolving the difficulties but no such thing has been done so far. In so serious a matter it does not become the revenue minister to persuade the people to participate in un-Islamic Capital investment by referring to it as an "Islamic duty".

It seems that the basic reason why no effective steps have been taken so far in this direction is that the government has no definite plan in its mind nor has the execution of the objective been entrusted to people possessing the required zeal and enthusiasm. Those who control the government's revenue schemes have done some superficial work as a covering up its declarations and then gone silent. They have neither drawn up any plan to move forward nor taken the trouble to look back at those departments which were to be purged of "interest" to see what is going on over there.

We desperately appeal to the government to review their performance on this subject. They have introduced themselves to the world as being dedicated to the implementation of the Shariah and, time and again, have broadcast their determination to mould their policies, laws and economy according to Islam. Therefore, it is time they fulfil their undertaking.

For the first time in the country's history a government has bound itself constitutionally to purge its departments of interest within three years. Two of the three years have already gone by without any positive action being taken, therefore, it devolves, constitutionally and morally, upon the government to purge its departments of "interest" within the remaining next year.

This will be possible only if those men are selected for executing the work who possess not only the ability and vision in revenue matters but are also endowed with the Islamic spirit and fervour to perform the required task of purging the country of "interest" as an important life objective.

If any difficulty comes across in the proposals made by the Council, it can be resolved with the assistance of the ulema and economic experts in accordance with the shariah. Strict supervision should be kept over the working of those organizations where interest is eliminated. As long as men of courage dedicated with determination to the achievement of success are not appointed to execute this task, this pressing need of our economic life will remain as it is, and this nation which, for thirty-five years, has been the victim of deception and fraudulent promises will despair also of the promises made by the present government. To expect such a nation to cooperate in national construction will only be self-illusion.

May Allah bestow on those in power the gift of right understanding to act upon it with courage, and also the will to fulfill the promises which are the only justification for their being where they are!

Muhammad Taqi Usmani

New Scheme of Musharika (Co-sharing)

Time and again has the present government announced its intention to reform the socio-economic structure according to Islamic principles. It has also publicly admitted that the basic cause of the economic mess gnawing into all its parts is "interest" of which it is determined as professed, to purge the national life.

In his inaugural address, after he had reshaped the Council of Islamic Ideology in 1977, President General Muhammed Zia ul Haq advised the members that they should give first priority to elimination of the curse of "interest". Accordingly, the council submitted its report to him within two years and the government announced that it wanted to see interest-free banking commence very soon.

After this announcement, the banks started new scheme for opening interest-free accounts. Although in our view, the running of interest-free accounts side by side of interest-bearing accounts was not proper, we studied the scheme very considerably, looking upon it as something being better than nothing. But we were distressed to find that the greater part of the scheme was exactly as before, a continuation of the erstwhile interest-bearing manner of banking and there was no difference between the one and the other, except a change of names.

We have criticized this scheme in al Balagh a number of times, proving that it does not correspond with Islamic principles.

On the occasion of the last Annual Budget, the revenue minister announced a new interest-free co-sharer scheme, giving the impression that the moneys of the profit and loss sharing account would be invested only in such commerce according to Islamic principles. The categorical announcement revised our hopes that, at least, the interest-free accounts would be purged of the curse of "interest". For long time the details of this new co-sharer scheme were not available to us, but when, at last, they did come, our fond hopes were shattered once again. The new scheme bearing the innocent name of co-sharing is only another form of interest-bearing and, in some respects, even worse!

The gist of the new scheme is that a business house desiring to borrow its capital from a bank should draw out a full plan of its project and invite a bank to become a partner for a temporary period. If the bank approves of the plan, it will provide the capital, the agreement stipulating the proportion of the profit of each of the two partners. But if the business suffers a loss, the bank will be reimbursed with the reserve held by it of the businessman's security, and if this does not make up for the bank's loss, the bank will appropriate to itself the businessman's share to the extent of its loss.

On the surface, the scheme seems to be correct, being based on the principle of sharing profit and loss, but what happens in case of loss is against the Shariah and is the worst possible form of "interest".

First, the business organization's reserve has nothing to do with the bank becoming a partner in the business, but is the saving of the house's former business. Second, it is an amazing condition that the lender should become the owner of whatever lies with it of the borrower's reserve. The difference between "interest" and co- sharing is that in the one the borrower's profit is uncertain while the lender's is guaranteed; the lender is not concerned in the least with any loss that the borrower may suffer whereas in co-sharing both the parties share simultaneously the prospects of profit as well as of loss.

The scheme is worse than the current interest system because, in the latter case, the lender has nothing to do with the borrower's fate after he gets his interest, but in the proposed scheme the lender not only gets his principal back but also becomes a permanent co-sharer of the profits which the other party may ever earn. The scheme is too exploitative, labelled as Islamic, it is a disgraceful fraud on the Muslims!

More than with a painful heart, we request the government to refrain from taking half-hearted measures. First, it was only "interest" to cry over, now it is fraud and deceit as well. We said repeatedly that the proposals of the Council of Islamic Ideology are before the government. If there are any difficulties, they can be removed by mutual discussion. On no account should the label of "interest-free" banking be affixed to interest-bearing transactions, because, doing this will be injurious here as well as in the hereafter!

As a whole we look upon General Zia ul Haq's government as comparatively better than any former government, and, therefore, we pray for his success with sympathy and sincerity, and, as far as possible, do not hesitate to cooperate with him. That is why such steps as this new scheme taken during his government pain us and doubts and misgivings arise. We pray Allah may grant it the understanding of the correct ways to implement the shariah and to face the difficulties on the way with courage!

Muhammad Taqi Usmani 18 JAMADI II 1403 AH.

Interest-free banking: some impressions

Glory be to him who gave shape and form this World and blessings be on the last of His Prophets who proclaimed the Truth!

Allah Has bestowed on Prince Muhammed al Faisal, the late Shah Faisal's son, a special fervour and enthusiasm to establish interest-free banking. He has worked assiduously for many years to establish such banks and has succeeded in his fervent efforts to do so in several parts of the world. At present, such banks are already operating in Dubai, Kuwait, Bahrain, Jordan, Egypt, Sudan, Geneva, and many other parts of the world. Their efforts are directed towards presenting a pattern of Islamic banking purged of interest in all its varieties.

Under his patronage and leadership, an International Association of Islamic Banks, too, has been established which coordinates the work of all such banks and assists them in every required way, especially, to resolve the difficulties that may arise in their practical work. There is also an ulema board, *al Riqabat ul Shariah al Mabnuk al Islamiah*, consisting of fifteen great ulema such as Shaykh Khatir, Shaykh Badr ul Mutawalli and Shaykh Yusuf al Qardwi, working under association. Its function is to analyse the working of the banks in the light of the Shariah and submit its advice whenever necessary.

These banks were independent of the other world banks and, therefore, constantly run into various difficulties to resolve which they have to work out new schemes with the ulema board reflects upon to submit its proposals for guidance.

On March 22, the Association held a convention at Islamabad to consider the problems of interest-free banking. A conference of the ulema board, *al Riqaba al Shariah*, was also held. As this author was invited to both, he had ample opportunity to study their working. The following are some of his impressions:

Besides Prince Muhammad al Faisal, the heads of the banks in various countries were present in the general sessions, some reading their papers in the light of their experiences with interest-free banking and some merely as observers. Heads of some of the bigger finance houses in Pakistan were also invited to attend.

The talks pre-eminently were on the subject whether "interest" could at all be included in Riba. There was a time when those influenced by the West believed that bank-interest was not Riba. That stage is now over. Finance and economic experts now concede that bank interest is very much to be included in the definition of Riba and is absolutely forbidden. The subject of the conferences held in Muslim countries is no longer whether bank interest is Riba, but how banking can be made interest-free.

Accordingly, this was the subject under consideration at the Islamabad Convention. The invitees were not conventional ulema but top experts on finance and banking. All of them dwelt on the pros and cons of interest-banking and interest-free banking and expressed their determination to produce a pattern of banking which, looked at entirely from the economics angle and yet remaining within Islamic limits, would be more beneficial and of wider range of influence.

Moreover, the fact that interest-free banks are working in several countries proves that elimination of interest from banking is no longer a polemic dream but a concrete reality. Of course, banks of the centuries old tradition are not likely to cooperate with our new pattern of banks which are bound to run into some practical difficulties, and it is also possible that there may still be some weak spots in their working from the Shariah and fiqh point of view, but it augurs well that the representative heads are agreed they will not be deterred by the intricacies and difficulties and are determined to overcome them; and that just as they will do their best to make a success of every scheme, so will they also try to remove the smallest defects in the light of fiqh legal requirements.

This, indeed, is a very auspicious beginning. If the work is continued with such zeal and enthusiasm, the results are bound to be encouraging. The Islamic banks are but a few among a myriad other, but one of the results already has been that even those countries are now thinking of interest-free banking the governments of which are entirely secular. Turkey has permitted interest-free banks to operate, while In Sudan interest-charging is no longer supported by law. If the process continues, the Islamic banks will not only be able to compete with interest-running banks but also be a pattern for them to adopt.

In his inaugural address, President General Muhammed Zia ul Haq said that what is basically needed for the implementation of the Shariah in the world of Islam is faith and belief in the heart. If there is trust in Allah and faith in His Mercy and Absolute Power, there is no obstacle in the way that cannot be overcome.

Quoting as example, he said that when prohibition was introduced in the country, liquor continued to be sold on PIA's overseas flights. Later, when it was announced that prohibition would extend to such flights also, it was said that PIA would suffer great financial losses. Nevertheless, prohibition was enforced as a religious duty, and by Allah's grace our flights, far from running on debit, are earning large profits.

He said that to put an end to interest-banking, the great need is to be firm in our belief that what Allah has decreed as forbidden cannot possibly be indispensable for us. If we work with such faith, every obstacle on the way will disappear, and we will attain our ultimate objective.

These thoughts of the President are laudable, indeed and very encouraging, as, in the same breath, he also announced that government was doing its best to put an end to interest-banking "as soon as possible".

While we appreciate these thoughts and announcements of the President, we cannot help recording our comments that whatever is being actually done at government level, no one at least, from among people like us, is able to see even a shadow of real work toward eliminating interest-banking. The sluggish speed with which things are going on the most fervent of the government's sympathizer find it difficult to believe that there will ever be an end to interest-loaded banking.

There has been no increase in the past three years in the number of the institutions that were purged of "interest" before, while new schemes have been coming one after the other which, except for the name, have no substance to them. From the Shariah angle, there is no difference between the interest-free counters and the usual interest counters. No effort, either has been made to bring the latter in line with the Shariah. We have repeatedly appealed that, at least, a joint meeting of the revenue officers and members of the Council should be called to consider the working of the interest-free counters so as to evolve a method to bring it in line with the Shariah. No such meeting has so far been convened. Everything is held in suspense; there is not even a gradual move towards the professed objective.

The President is right in saying that the basic need for eliminating interest is unshakable faith. The mind nurtured in the materialistic environments of the West will always try to frighten us with its statistics. But if our faith is truly firm that Allah's commands are binding on us, whatever the price involved, and that He does not make us suffer unnecessarily, the practical experiment is bound to dispel the nightmares.

The President has very rightly quoted the example of PIA's overseas flights. Had government allowed itself to be intimidated by statistical figures, such flights would still have been contaminated with strong liquor. But when full trust was placed in Allah and determined efforts were made, the world saw how Allah's assistance come to help.

So, with the subject of interest-free banking, as long as we desist from such faith and do not work with the same ardent fervour, our economy will never be freed of the tentacles of the ogre that interest is. Lately, a member of the Sudanese executive, Dr. Hasan Iltizabi, came to Pakistan and he told me personally that it has been announced in his country that if banks want to carry on with interest- bearing transactions, they may do so on their own responsibility, but the law Courts will not sanction them. This announcement was made long ago but the skies have not fallen for that reason. If Sudan can take this bold step, why cannot Pakistan, the foundation of which is said to be Islam?

All this should not be taken as criticism for the sake of criticism but to draw the government's attention that administrative power is a great trust from Allah. This trust does not remain in one's hands forever. Allah has provided the President with an opportunity to implement the Shariah and has also given with it a sufficient period of time for the purpose. If the President avails of this opportunity in the right way, at least, to relieve the country of "interest", it will redound to his credit in this life and the Hereafter, and this nation which does want to live under an Islamic order, will pray for him. But if he does not avail of the opportunity in the right manner, he will be held severely answerable. Therefore, he should, without wasting any further time, set himself very resolutely to the task of relieving the nation of the curse of "interest". Allah's help will be with him. The Quran has equated "interest" with "war with Allah and His Prophet ﷺ". As long as we do not repent of this war, we shall not deserve Allah's mercy; but if once we make up our minds from the core of our hearts not to rest until we have put an end to this treacherous "war with Allah and His Prophet "whatever the cost, the happy news from Allah is: "If they have faith and fear Allah (*taqwa*), We shall open the bountiful doors of the skies on them."

May Allah bestow on us the treasure of faith that we shall trample upon every obstacle that comes in the way of carrying out His commands and obeying them in our private and collective lives, avert His wrath and, perchance, deserve of His Mercies! - Aameen.

Muhammad Taqi Usmani 26 Jamadi- us- Sani 1404 A.H.

Total end to "Interest"

New announcement of the Revenue Minister

Glory be to Him Who gave shape and form to this world and blessings be on the Last of His Prophets who proclaimed the Truth!

We would like to record in these pages some comments on the speech of the Revenue Minister, Mr. Ghulam Ishaq Khan.

The respected Minster has said that with reference to the last date October 1985, fixed by the President General Muhammed Zia ul Haq for eliminating "interest-banking", it has been decided to do so a few months earlier, namely by July 1985. No bank, after this date, shall conduct its business on the basis of "interest".

There may be differences of opinion in respect of the date, but everyone, without exception, who wishes to see Islamic teachings and commands implemented here, welcomes the glad tidings. Our ears had been waiting impatiently to hear them, and now, at last, they have come!

But because of our past experience with similar announcements in this connection, the tidings are not clear of doubts and misgivings, and questions arise in the minds of those who wish to see a purely Islamic order prevail.

As soon as the present government took over the reins of power, it included very prominently the elimination of interest-banking among its chief priority on the list of its many announcements. Thus, when the Council of Islamic Ideology was reshaped in 1977, the President, in his inaugural address, laid great stress on the need for working out the details for that purpose. At the time, I too was a member of the Council, and the President's profound concern in this matter was a source of great joy not only for us but throughout the country for everyone. This was the first time that a head of state had attached any importance to the subject when none before him had taken the trouble even to give a few minutes to the subject, and some had gone to length of stating that "interest" was not only permissible but indispensable to the country's economy.

Encouraged by the President's concern the Council set itself with great enthusiasm to work out a plan for a non-interest economy. It appointed a special panel comprising economic experts and representatives of the bankers and, in due course of time prepared a detailed Report, which it submitted, to the President.

After this, the government announced that non-interest counters would be opened in all the banks. Although we did not approve the interest-free counters and interest-counters working side by side, clients were allowed the option to use permissible or the impermissible---, we thought that something was better than nothing, there was no harm if the government looked up this as the first step towards an interest-free economy.

But when the details of this scheme came before us, we were sorely disappointed to find that the same spirit pervaded both the counters. We have previously recorded our arguments in full detail in the pages of al Balagh. Now, when the total elimination of interest-banking has been announced, suspicions do arise whether the result will be the same that befell the PLS Accounts: a change of names and no more. If so, there could be no greater tragedy for the national economy.

The success of interest-free banking lies in the satisfaction of the Muslims feeling that they may participate in it with the feeling that the scheme is not mixed up with impermissible earnings and is quite pure and in accordance with the Shariah. Such satisfaction cannot be brought about by superficialities. Not that the government has expressed its firm intention to make banking entirely interest- free, it should also be determined not the repeat the mistakes that, from the Shariah point of view, destroyed the PLS Accounts scheme.

The Revenue Minister's announcement of the date, July 1985 for ending interest-banking is to be welcomed. If the intention is not merely to change the name but to root out the evil from the national economy, the country must be relieved of the present system of PLS Accounts but if the idea is to expand the system to all bank accounts and yet look upon it as elimination of "interest", it will be no less than a fraud on the people.

We have, time and again, presented our proposal that the PLS Accounts scheme should be reconsidered jointly by the Ministry of Finance and the Council of Islamic Ideology so as to modify it according to the Shariah but, we regret, that to this day no action has been taken on this proposal.

The media reports news of joint sittings of the Ministry and economic experts and of the many things they settled but we do not know who the Ministry's advisers are that determine the Shariah validity of any scheme. What should have been done according to principle was to take the Council of Islamic Ideology into confidence and promote the work by its cooperation, but, as far as we know, the government has kept itself aloof from the Council and consultations with it have been deemed unnecessary.

Today, although the Council no longer exists as such, its period being over, (it should be revived) --- its former members are still alive, and the economic experts are well known. Every new scheme, free of Shariah defects, can be finalized by consulting them.

We draw the government's attention once again and call upon it to guarantee at the time of implementing the new interest-free structure that it will be one-hundred per cent according to Islamic principles, clear of the least taint. There still is time for the government to convince itself as well as create the necessary confidence among the masses that the new structure is dependable. It will not be a pleasant situation if the government keep announcing the total elimination of interest, and the country's ulema and other knowledgeable authorities, instead of welcoming the announcement, proclaim their denunciation of it.

Finally drawing the government's attention, we have done our duty. It is now up to the government to choose its options for bringing about the desired changes in the present social order. Will it permit the interest monster to continue pervading the millat and itself by subject to the anger and hatred of the Muslims or will it resort to such means as will factually relieve them of the curse, the people praying for those instrumental in relieving them of it. Power does not rest permanently with anyone, but blessed are those who use their position and authority to invoke Allah's pleasure. Mercies will, indeed, rain upon them who relieve the people of that war with Allah which He and His Prophet have threatened them with!

We pray that Allah bestow on those in authority the wisdom of making right decisions and the sincerity and true fervour to put a real end to the curse of interest instead of merely changing its name.

Muhammed Taqi Usmani 28 Shawwal 1404 AH..

Interest-free Banking: Government's latest auspicious measures

In the Zi Qa'd 1404 publication of this journal we recorded comments on Finance Minister Ghulam Ishaq Khan's our announcement at the time of his presenting the Annual Budget that interest-banking would be totally ended by July 1985. Welcoming the announcement we also expressed our doubts, common to many people, that if the procedure adopted was going to be the same as that in respect of PLS Accounts, it would again be nothing more than a change of names.

Our criticism was based on that part of his budget speech, which was published in the daily Jang of June 15, 1984. But later we learnt that Jang had not published the whole speech in that issue though the Minister had spoken in great detail about his plan and implementation procedure. We, therefore, secured the full speech and found that our comments needed to be corrected.

The first noteworthy point which we feel gratified about is that commencing from the current financial year those defects of the PLS Accounts which had made the scheme only another form of "interest" had been removed. He admitted that the learned authorities had pointed out those defects and shown that they were unacceptable from the Shariah point of view.

Some explanation may be necessary. When in January 1981 the government for the first time directed all banks to open Profit & Loss Accounts, we said, after studying the scheme, that it was but another form of "interest" and to style it as "interest-free" was not correct. Our comments were published in al Balagh of Rabi II 1401 AH and were reproduced in several journals and copies were sent to the various government departments.

We said that the only alternative to adopt after putting an end to interest-banking was Mudarbah, profit and loss sharing or free loans (*qard-e-hasana*). But where this was not possible in some of the bank's transactions, some other ways may be had recourse to.

One such way was *bai muajjal* or sale on deferred payment basis. That is, a bank may purchase a commodity for the borrower of capital and, charging a profit, sell it to him allowing him to pay the price at a later, agreed, date.

This is called "Mark Up". The Shariah permits this method, provided the bank actually purchases the commodity and sells it, albeit at a profit. Until now this method was not used in the permissible manner. First, the bank, instead of buying the relevant commodity and then selling it, gave the money to its client to acquire the commodity but to assume that the commodity had been bought by the bank and then sold to him. The price was to be paid according to an arranged ratio, Mark Up, within a fixed time. What this really amounted to was that there was no actual commodity trade but merely exchange of price money. The bank never possessed the commodity nor delivered it to the client. It was also stipulated that the price would be increased and would continue to be increased if it were not paid up by the agreed date. This was styled "Mark Up Upon Mark Up".

It is obvious that his was "interest", though the name was changed. We wrote:

> *"What can this procedure be but interest? How can an interest-free structure be established if interest were called Mark Up but all the features of interest remained intact?"*

We also demanded,

> *"Wherever Mark Up is indispensable the requirements of the Shariah must be fulfilled. That is, the conditions for increasing the Mark Up rate, when the price is not paid within the agreed date should be abolished, because the Shariah does not countenance such a condition. And it should be clearly stipulated that the commodity sold under Mark Up shall be sold after the bank takes possession of it.'*

(Al Balagh Rabi II 1401 AH. Pp.9 and 13)

Since 1401 AH until today we have been asserting and reasserting through the various media in a number of ways and under different headings that the Mark Up method, as practised has serious defects, and now, at last, the Revenue Minister has announced:

> *"Form the Shariah point of view a number of objections were made to the Mark Up method as included in the PLS scheme. In consequence of these objections, that method is to be abolished. Instead, the bank or whatever, will refer to a tribunal, established specially for the purpose to make action after summary hearing."*

(Budget speech pp.25, 26)

In compliance with this speech, the State Bank of Pakistan advised all banks to alter their rules accordingly. The State Bank News of July 1, 1984 explained:

> *"The bank will buy the commodity and then sell it to its client at a reasonable Mark Up and no Mark Up on this. Mark Up will be permitted."*

(Vol. 23, No. 13, p.1, col.2)

The improvement in the Mark Up system will prove auspicious in the future.

Another scheme titled Musharika was launched in the PLS Accounts, but it pained us to find that only the name was correct while "interest" was retained as before. Commenting in detail on this scheme it was wrote in Al Balagh of Rajab 1403:

> *"The truth is that this scheme too is the worst form of exploitation and interest, to implement which in the name of Islam is a disgraceful fraud on the Muslims."* (p. 5)

Under this scheme a bank becomes a co-sharer in the temporary business programme of a trading house and if the business undergoes a loss the bank will first be reimbursed from the security, and if the loss is not fully compensated, the bank will be deemed automatically to have become the owner of the client's shares to the extent of the remaining loss. It is obvious that placing the entire burden of the loss on the client completely destroys the whole spirit of partnership. We wrote:

> *"For God's sake, refrain from these half-hearted efforts. Before, there was only the sin of interest transactions, now the sin committing a fraud on the Muslims may also be added to it."* (P. 5)

We are grateful and happy that the revenue minister has announced in his speech to eliminate this method of partnership. He said:

> *"These methods have been used before in certain situations; now their use will be extended on a larger canvas. The defect existing at present in the Musharika and Participation Term Certificate, namely, that the whole burden of the loss will be borne entirely by the business house, will be done away because it is un-Islamic, as pointed out by a number of intellectuals."*

(Budget speech p.26)

The fact that changes have been made in the Mark Up and co-sharing schemes on the demand of the intellectuals has brought us a double cause for satisfaction. One, the country has been relieved of "interest" as far as these schemes are concerned; second, the government has not insisted on continuing its mistake but by accepting constructive advice has established a precedent. So far, the excuse made was that the counsels did not come from professionals and, therefore, could not be done the basis of far-reaching policies in respect of such delicate matters as finance. Yet another cause for our satisfaction is that these reforms show that the announcement of July 1. 1985 regarding the elimination of interest by the same day, July 1, 1985, is serious and the government is really taking positive steps in the right direction.

In his speech, the Revenue Minister also announced the relevant programme:

> *"As we promised last year, a concrete programme has been drawn up in consultation with the State Bank and national commercial banks to put a total end to "interest". This programme, effective from the next revenue year will apply to all banks and finance organizations, including the foreign banks operating in Pakistan."* (P. 5)

"This programme is as follows: -

1) "From the 1st of January 1985 every instruction sent by the government to corporations, joint stock companies and banks, whether public or private, shall be in accordance with Islamic rules. The transitory period of six months allowed (before January 1) is necessary to enable alterations to be made in the laws and rules, normalize new accounts keeping methods, provide the necessary training to bank employees, and make other necessary preparations.

2) "From April 1, 1985, tamveel to individuals and firms will be altered strictly and totally according to the Shariah. In this way, the direction of the Assets of banks and other financial organizations will be altered to comply with Islamic Rules. Only the previous agreements will need to be fulfilled."
3) "Commencing July 1, 1985, all banks shall not accept deposits on interest. All savings and transitory Accounts shall stand altered according to Islam. Only the current Accounts will operate as at present."
4) "The Islamic requirements shall be extended to the agricultural and cooperative organizations also."
5) "All matters concerning the State Bank, whether connecting with the government or commercial banks shall be according to Islam".

We would like to congratulate the government on these auspicious decisions and pray that Allah Subhana-Hu wa Ta'la may grant them the will and courage to purge the national economic structure of the curse of interest, without mental reservations of any kind and without being overawed by any extraneous thought, and to remove any defects that may yet remain so that they may pave the way to a truly Islamic economic social order!

In his speech, the revenue minister has also indicated the different ways in which interest-bearing transactions will be eliminated, and, in compliance, the State Bank has sent a circular of instructions to all banks. These instructions have been published in the State Bank News of July 1, 1984.

Alongside, because of some practical difficulties, the Revenue Minister also requested the ulema and other authorities to furnish their answers to some questions.

We believe that it is the duty of the ulema to study very carefully all the matters via media that have been proposed for the new order, and, if there are drawbacks in them from the Shariah point of view, they should sent to the government their views and proposals as well as their replies to the questions in time so that efforts may be made to remove the defects before July 1.

We shall give the proposed details of interest-free banking and our comments on the Revenue Minister's questions at some later date. For the present we have three suggestions to offer.

First, that the necessary condition for Mark Up being that the bank must actually sell the commodity in question to its client, and not merely give him the money to purchase it, it shall no longer be permissible to assume that the bank has sold it to him. Although the State Bank Circular has clarified this mentioning regular "buying and selling", because banks have been in the habit of following the other practice, it is necessary to remind them again with due emphasis.

Second: the State Bank Circular mentions the purchase of Trade Bills as one of the procedural methods and states that it will be on the basis of Mark Down, which, in fact, means that the method of cashing in of Bills of Exchange and hundis will be the same as already current; the only difference will be a change of names, "Mark Down" instead of "Discount".

This does not seem to be acceptable from the Shariah point of view. We suggest that just as the details of Mark Up have been changed, the method of cashing Bills of Exchange should also be changed. The Council's Report for eliminating interest includes a proposal in this regard which should be tried. Difficulties, if any, can be resolved by mutual discussion but to continue with the current practice is not justifiable.

Third: in connection with the Participation Term Certificate, it is stated in the Revenue Minister's speech and the State Bank Circular that the maximum and minim profit rate will be fixed from time to time by the State Bank, but the loss will be borne by both the parties in proportion to the capital invested by each of them.

There is no harm done if this means that the State Bank shall fix the percentage rate of the profit due to the banks from the collective profits, because this is the most effective way in which the State Bank will be able to exercise its control over the currency rate. But it will be objectionable if this means that the State Bank should fix the maximum and minimum profit according to the investment.

The words "Rates of Profit" used in the Circular, may raise the suspicion that this latter is intended, and the intention is to make the participating client feel secure that the profits above the limit fixed by the State Bank will be allotted to him and not to the bank concerned... If this is what is really meant by fixing the rate of profit, it is unjustified in the Shariah and, besides, no benefit can the interest-free structure do to the economy.

The great benefit of *Mudarbah* or participation is that the system contributes to balancing the social distribution of wealth, while interest-loaded transactions cause the whole of the greater part of the profit to go to one party and, in case of loss, the whole loss is wholly that of one party. By conducting banking according to participation *Mudarbah* principles, the entire profits, when great, do not accrue only to the investing client but, through the bank, to the general public as well. Inflation is controlled, the lower-class incomes are increased, and idle currency circulates, with better all- round effects on the whole economy.

That is why it is forbidden in the Shariah to stipulate that in case of extra profits, they will not be allotted to the bank. This may be good news for the capitalist or investor but the benefits consequent upon complying with Islamic commands, the better balancing of wealth distribution, are narrowed down.

May it be that this is not what the government intends! Otherwise, we emphatically have to say that this will negate the entire interest-free structure, and should, therefore, be altered. However, in order to retain the State Bank control, the division ratio of the profits due to each party should be stipulated.

With these appeals we welcome the measures taken by the government.

Muhammed Taqi Usmani 23 Muharram ul Haram 1405 AH

New Budget and Interest-Bearing Schemes

All praise for Him Who created this world and all salutation for His last Messenger who disseminated the truth.

New budget for the next fiscal year was presented in National Assembly this month. There are various debatable issues in this budget but firstly it requires technical knowledge to comment on it, which I do not claim to have nor does it relate to our subject; secondly, though many aspects of this budget relate to our main structure but they require a detailed discussion, which is out of place here!

There is only one aspect of the budget, which is directly related our subject, and government policy in this regard was awaited since long.

The government had promised in the beginning of the last fiscal year that during the current year, element of interest would be purged of from economy. A stage-wise programme was announced according to which interest was to be eliminated from economy from 1st of July 1985. Therefore, the new budget was supposed to have contained the steps taken by the government in this regard.

As far as the banking system is concerned, we have frequently submitted in the previous pages that the system devised for it contains lot of defects, from, religious point of view. Out of twelve modes devised by the State Bank as replacement to the interest some of them are permissible according to Shariah, but some of them are equivocal, some categorically invalid and still some which are in fact other forms of interest. Details will be dealt with in future Allah willing.

But the second important issue regarding elimination of interest is the saving schemes which are introduced by the government for getting benefit from the savings of the public and interest is given on them, e.g.

Prize Bonds, Defence Saving Certificates, Term Deposit Certificates, etc. According to the last year's announcement, the government was under an obligation to eliminate interest on these schemes from the current fiscal year and to bring them within parameters of Shariah.

The practical problem faced by the government was that should the interest be eliminated from these schemes, and the bearers of these schemes are returned the same amount they have invested, the people may show disinterest in them and may withdraw their amounts; and the huge amount from the income of government may reduce or even terminate.

But obviously, the one year's time taken by the government on the occasion of the last budget, was meant to find the solution to this problem in the meanwhile, according to the principles of Shariah. Therefore, these were the only two options for the government viz. if the government had found solution, these schemes should have been modified and if it could not have paid due attention to this problem, it should, at least, have declared that it has not yet devised alternative schemes, so it may be given some more time.

But the comments of the finance minister published in newspapers in this regard were a source of great astonishment and worry. According to the media reporting, he has said, "This scheme does not contain element of interest and religious scholars have also been consulted in this regard." The question is that if these schemes do not contain interest, then on what grounds it was announced last year to eliminate interest from them? We do not know those scholars who have declared these schemes interest-free. But it someone has declared their fluctuated sale as valid by declaring financial instruments as trade items, then he should also have announced that the interest does not even exist on this earth and thus making every interest-bearing transaction as valid through inflated sale of loan document.

The new finance minister has said on a number of occasions that he does not intend to adopt such method for elimination of interest which would be just a formal documentation, and if he could not find an alternative system which is in accordance with the Shariah, he would simply declare that he requires further time.

In this perspective, we were stunned to read in newspapers that these schemes do not contain elements of interest. This explanation is so poor that we fell in doubt that whether or not the comments of the concerned minister were reported correctly.

Nevertheless, if the reporting is correct, then it is very shameful to continue with these interest-bearing schemes by declaring them interest free. There is still some time in the implementation of the budget, and if this time is not utilized in rectifying this serious mistake, it will prove a slur for that government which is in power in the name of Islam.

As stated earlier, we had a doubt about the authenticity regarding the reporting of the comments of the finance minister, but later on, an explanatory statement of the said minister has been published in newspapers which further strengthened our doubt. His statement shows that he has not yet declared anything with certainty regarding the religious position of these schemes, rather has decided to refer the issue to a committee of scholars.

This second news has, no doubt, reduced the grave impact left by the previous reporting, but this news is also ambiguous about the real issue; because it does not disclose whether or not the government intends to rectify these schemes in near future.

We humbly submit that this issue is hanging unresolved for many years and the practical contradiction found in the official announcements and steps taken thereof, have adversely impaired the trust of the government regarding enforcement of Shariah. This situation is undesirable for any government, particularly for the government whose very existence is based on the promise of enforcement of Shariah. So, this issue needs to be resolved at the earliest and instead of setting up long term committees and commissions, what is required is to hold a few days' sitting in which the finance ministry should present their practical problems before reliable scholars and their religious solution be found through mutual consideration and understanding. The only pre-requisite is the sincerity and faith, that they have gathered to find a solution to an issue which has been declared by Allah as unlawful and a "war against Allah and His Prophet (Peace be upon him)"; if this would be the passion, then within no time deliverance from this curse could be sought.

The new finance minister is internationally acknowledged for his profound insight and vast experience in the field of economics. It is also said about him that instead of following the example of any other country, he is always in pursuit of exploring new dimensions, and the new budget is also reflective of it. If in a country like Pakistan, which was founded in the name of religion, his God gifted skill is utilized in transforming economy in Islamic structure, would not only be a source of honour for him but will be a good, sign for the country as well. It is cordially prayed that may Allah bestow him with honour and courage to perform this great obligation.

Aameen

Muhammad Taqi Usmani

15 Ramadan ul Mubarik 1405 AH

www.ingramcontent.com/pod-product-compliance
Lightning Source LLC
Chambersburg PA
CBHW050528240926
51846CB00003B/741
9788119946761